RESTORING SCHOOL CIVILITY

Creating a caring, responsible, and productive school

Dr. Philip F. Vincent
with Dr. David Wangaard and Paul Weimer

Restoring School Civility: Creating a Caring, Responsible, and Productive School

Publisher: Character Development Group, Inc.
366 Bella Vista Dr., Boone, NC 28607
828-355-9494
E-mail: Info@CharacterEducation.com
www.CharacterEducation.com

Text editing by Ginny Turner
Layout by Sara Sanders, SHS Design

ISBN: 1-892056-22-4
$22.95

Printed in the United States of America

Acknowledgments

Several years ago I wrote a small book entitled *Rules and Procedures for Character Education: The First Step Toward School Civility* (1999). It was written in response to requests to expand my concept that consistent rules and procedures are essential for developing schools of character. In the book, I argued that rules were to act as social and moral guideposts and the procedures were to be the practices that would eventually develop in students and teachers habits of civility. Many educators who used the book reported it was helpful for developing consistency in promoting expectations and habits of civility in their schools. Although it was manifestly useful, I was not satisfied that is was a complete enough statement concerning the why's and how's of promoting school civility. For example, it didn't mention the importance of the teacher being the moral compass of the classroom and all the adults being the moral compass throughout the school. Neither did it include how to use the curriculum itself in developing the civil school. It was time to keep what was valuable in *Rules and Procedures* but rethink the entire notion of school civility.

I had shared some initial writing and ideas with two of my good friends, David Wangaard and Paul Weimer. David and I had both worked in education in Alaska—I as a teacher in Valdez and Palmer, and David as a principal in Anchorage. Although Alaska has a small state educator population, we never met, but through various professional meetings involving character education after we had both returned to "the lower 48" we got to know each other professionally and then on a personal level. I explained to David my original thoughts and he reminded me that serving others—sacrificing the wants of the individual for the needs of others—is an important part of any civil society and that includes the civil school. He was right, so I asked him if he'd write a chapter on how serving others can promote a civil school. David agreed and wrote the chapter on service learning and also provided many insights on my work in the other chapters.

I met Paul Weimer while he was assistant director at the Georgia Humanities Council, in charge of character education. Paul has a wonderful, diverse academic background. He speaks with intelligence and insight in most areas of the humanities. I asked Paul if he would contribute an introduction and assist on the chapter concerning the use of the humanities in promoting school civility. Paul agreed to do this despite a recent marriage and a move to Washington, D.C.! I could not be associated with any better thinkers and friends. You guys are great!

This work also was influenced by the insights and conversations of many people. I especially want to thank "Marvelous" Marvin Berkowitz for always pushing me to think deeper about my assumptions and assertions. Marvin is a world renowned educator and the Sanford N. McDonnell Professor of Character Education at the University of Missouri–St. Louis. How he finds time for me I will never know, but I do appreciate our professional and personal relationship and I do not hold him responsible for my incomplete thinking!

I also wish to thank Deb Brown, Thomas Lickona, Matt Davidson, Norman Sprinthall, John Arnold, Darcia Narvaez, Helen LeGette, Linda McKay, Ed DeRoche, Jerry Corley, Kevin Ryan, Avis Glaze, Alice Loeb, Hal Urban, Joe Hester, Nancy Reed, Lisa Burton, Donna Cianfrani, Darcy Kempt, Steve Dixon, Ivan Crissman, Charlie Abourjilie, Betty Hensley, Bonnie Henry, and Janet Cates for their powerful writings and/or insights into the social and moral development of children. I appreciate all of you on a professional and personal level. I also apologize to you in advance as I know I haven't presented your ideas as completely as possible.

My associates at the Character Development Group are the finest people and friends one could work with, or for that matter call friends. We built this company on a handshake and vowed to act with integrity in all our dealings with each other. What started out as business partners have now become wonderful friends. Dixon Smith, Penny Smith, and Stacy Shelp-Peck's commitment to the social and moral development of children is what drives our mission and our friendship. I am a very lucky man to work with you.

Finally, I must thank my wife Cynthia and daughter Mary Kathryn. You kept the home fires burning while I was traveling from Canada to California to Florida and all states in between. Although I may not say it enough, I love you both with all my heart. Indeed, you are my heart.

Philip Vincent
June 2004

Preface

Before reading the body of the work, consider the following taken from a recent report (May 2004) concerning school civility. Public Agenda, with support from Common Good, surveyed 725 middle and high school teachers and 600 parents of middle and high school students. (Their report is available for free download at: www.publicagenda.org.) Among the findings are:

- Both teachers and parents agree that a part of a school's mission—in addition to the academics—is to teach kids to follow the rules so they can become productive citizens (93% and 88%).

- Both groups show high levels of support for the "broken windows" approach—strictly enforcing the little rules so the right tone is created and bigger problems are avoided: 61% for the teachers and 63% of parents strongly support this, with another 30% of teachers and 25% of parents supporting this idea somewhat.

- Most teachers believe putting more of an emphasis on classroom management skills in teacher education programs would go a long way toward improving student discipline and behavior: 54% say this would be a very effective solution and another 37% somewhat effective.

The time is now! Some may be reading and using this book as part of teacher education but the great majority of readers will be administrators and teachers who are searching for a better school life for their students and their coworkers. Only by acting now can we preserve the dream of a quality education for all our children. This will demand that we think and rethink our old paradigms and assumptions. Leaving no child behind will require that efforts in promoting a civil school be treated as seriously as our academic efforts. Let us begin with intent and effort. The future of our schools may well rest on our efforts!

Over the last 15 years I have traveled to schools and districts
throughout the United States and Canada.
It has been a true blessing to work with so many caring educators.
I am so much fulfilled as a person due to your insights and kindness.
With pleasure, I dedicate this book to you.

Table of Contents

Introduction

BY PAUL WEIMER

Civility is a word many of us associate only with good manners and common courtesies. But an exploration of the variety of associations tied to the word can lead us on an interesting path that binds together the school, the community, and the larger world in ways that have important implications for all. According to the *The American Heritage® Dictionary of the English Language*, 4th edition (2000), *civility* is defined as:

"Everyone take your seats! Let's try to act civilized for just a few moments!"

> **NOUN: 1. Courteous behavior;** politeness. 2. A courteous act or utterance.

What is the larger meaning of a book about civility in the school? Obviously, we would all like to work in a setting marked by courteous behavior and politeness, as indeed, we would like to live in a world marked by the same. We believe that the establishment of courteous and polite behavior is essential in developing the civil school, as well as the civil society. But thinking of this simple definition does not capture the scope of what we envision when we imagine such a world or workplace.

Let's take, for example, a scene that many of us have seen or heard—a lunchroom or study hall or classroom in utter chaos. An exasperated voice rises above the din and calls for order: "Everyone take your seats! Let's try to act *civilized* for just a few moments!" Such a call makes an impression, even if it is met with mild amusement. On the other hand, a call for "civility" might make an impression, but would also very likely draw its share of blank stares, even though a call for a return to courteous behavior and politeness makes sense in a chaotic setting. So let's also consider the word *civilized*:

> **ADJECTIVE: 1. Having a highly developed society and culture.** 2. Showing evidence of moral and intellectual advancement; humane, ethical, and reasonable. 3. Marked by refinement in taste and manners; cultured; polished.

If we take the latter two definitions first, we see that both point to positive behaviors, with the last being more closely tied to the courteous acts suggested in the definition of civility. It is easier to conduct our lives when those around us have these attributes. The second definition suggests an even higher level of behavior, tying together reasoning, ethics, and moral and intellectual advancement. We also want to be around adults and children who are reasonable and who, when the time demands it, are capable of intellectual and moral pursuits. Therefore, can we assume that the first definition, "having a highly developed society or culture," is tied to the second and third definitions? We believe it is, and we feel that definitions two and three support the eventual goal of living in a society of good culture.

Now let's consider the root word of both of the two words we have examined, *civil*:

> **ADJECTIVE: 1. Of, relating to, or befitting a citizen or citizens:** *civil duties.* 2. Of or relating to citizens and their interrelations with one another or with the state: *civil society; the civil branches of government.* 3. Of ordinary citizens or ordinary community life as distinguished from the military or the ecclesiastical: *civil authorities.* 4. Of or in accordance with organized society; civilized. 5. Sufficiently observing or befitting accepted social usage; not rude: *a civil reply.* See synonyms at *polite.* 6. Being in accordance with or denoting legally recognized divisions of time: *a civil year.* 7. *Law* Relating to the rights of private individuals and legal proceedings concerning these rights as distinguished from criminal, military, or international regulations or proceedings. ETYMOLOGY: Middle English, from Latin *civilis,* from *civis,* citizen. See *civic.*

With definition number four, "Of or in accordance with organized society; civilized," we see an immediate tie to the teacher's outburst where we began. We can quickly translate our teacher's remark thus: "Let's try to act as if we are members of an organized society!" This is likely the sense of the word that is best understood by students, even if only vaguely. The call to "act civilized" is amusing because the larger reality, which our students do indeed grasp, is that they live in and attend school in a civilized society, one that is organized under the rule of law.

A school is a microcosm of organized society with its own principles governing the interactions of its members.

Looking further at the word above, we see that definition five points us toward positive behaviors and courtesies by the obverse: "not rude." There is also a key phrase here, "accepted social usages," that we should mark for a moment for further consideration below.

But first, the school is naturally a representation of our membership in organized society, established as a means for information and knowledge to be transferred, learned, and discovered in an organized fashion from one generation to the next. This applies not only to the obligatory academic pursuits, but also to the habits of civility which are essential to living a good life. A school is also a microcosm of organized society with its own principles governing the interactions of its members. Schools have codes of conduct and discipline and sometimes have dress codes or other standards that outline the boundaries of appropriate behavior, just as our municipalities, counties, and states have codes of law to govern behavior. This is what we see in definition two above: "the interrelations of citizens to one another and to the state."

In this important respect, the smaller community of our school mirrors the structure of our larger communities—they are ordered in such a way as to govern how individuals relate to one another and to the whole. The seriousness with which we regard that order in the school has profound implications for how our students come to understand the structures and prohibitions that govern our interrelations beyond the school. Through the organization of school life our students learn lessons about respecting authority, justice (and its application), and a host of concepts that prepare them for citizenship—for being a member of a state and appreciating what it means to live in an organized society.

Generally speaking, the kinds of behaviors that appear in a school's conduct code are the exception rather than the rule in day-to-day classroom scenes. It is safe to say that most students are knowledgeable enough of the prohibitions in these codes to have heard or have internalized that "we're not supposed to do that" when confronted by a restricted behavior, even if they may engage in it. But knowing what we're *not* supposed to do does not necessarily suggest we know what we *are* supposed to do. Indeed, no one is programmed from birth to use the behaviors that are the hallmark of civility—such behaviors are *learned* by observation and practice.

What are the settings in which this kind of learning and practice takes place? This brings us back to the phrase "accepted social usages" that we noted in the definition of *civil* above. While laws in our communities and school conduct codes proscribe certain behaviors, do they list "accepted social usages," that is, appropriate and desirable behaviors governing the interactions of our members? Certainly affirmations of positive behaviors abound, from the Boy Scout Laws to the creeds in faith communities of all kinds. But they stand alone in a flood of examples and affirmations of less desirable and undesirable behaviors surrounding our youth. Students see, hear, and absorb these latter behaviors from peer groups and the media, even the home.

Within this milieu of disparate, not-always-positive influences, the school stands as the most commonly shared experience and institution for most of our youth. For some young people it may be an island of refuge because of its order and routine in an otherwise troubling sea of confusion. For all, it should stand as a bridge leading not only to new knowledge and information, but also to understanding and skills to engage successfully in the varied human interaction of the larger world of organized society. Fundamental to this interaction is the ability to respect both the prohibitions and strictures of the law (e.g., stop at red lights) and the less articulated positive behaviors (e.g., wait your turn exiting the stadium parking lot) that smooth social interaction and allow

The school stands as the most commonly shared experience and institution for most of our youth.

us to live our lives safely and predictably. As a bridge institution, the school stands as a mediator of accepted social usage. The school environment, with the behaviors it prohibits and those it actively models and promotes, is a microcosm of the larger world of work and society. The school can serve as a greenhouse for nurturing and growing in young people the healthy and productive habits of social, moral, and intellectual pursuits that make organized, civilized society possible.

Civility in the school is a phrase with varied nuances and multiple implications for our interactions within the school and society at large. This book is intended to introduce a broader appreciation of these implications at several levels and to suggest strategies, practices, and opportunities for instilling or restoring civility in our schools.

CHAPTER 1

Considerations of Civility

Our daily life consists of a series of interactions with other people—our neighbors, coworkers, students, and bosses, plus various strangers in stores, restaurants, and offices whose paths we cross. Few of these individuals are at the heart of our lives, but if an interaction with one of them is sour, it can adversely color our day. Consider the following scenarios:

- You are driving to work and are unable to move over to allow another driver into your lane. Soon this driver, who merged several cars later, pulls up beside your car and starts blowing her horn. As you look over, you notice the driver shouting at you and displaying an obscene gesture.

- In a store, you are unable to find the product you need. You see that several clerks are standing around, casually talking to their friends, unaware that you need help. When you make your purchase, the clerk does not look at you or even thank you for your business.

- You attend a soccer match and notice several parents in the stands screaming at the referees. After the game, one father goes on the field and pushes a referee. Luckily, a coach sees this and steps between the parent and the referee. The father is arrested and charged with assault.

- You watch a political talk show on TV, but all you can hear is the hosts yelling at and browbeating their guests. Interruptions and rudeness overshadow what is being said.

- A teacher enters a classroom and is greeted by a student who says, "Hey, my man. What's up?" The class does not quiet down. Another student shouts an obscenity at a classmate. Still another student calls out to remind a girl that they are to meet for lunch. The classroom's chaotic behavior is not directed only toward the teacher—disrespectful language, facial and physical gestures are directed toward the other students. Several days later, an assistant principal comes into the room to talk with the class about their behavior. When he mentions the word "civility," the class responds that they are civil—they like the class "just the way it is" and they explode in laughter. Behavior in this classroom is the norm at this school.

- In another school, a principal reports that the students regularly throw paper down in front of the custodian and tell him, "It's your job to clean up our mess." They have also told teachers, "My parents make more in a month than you make in a year. It doesn't really matter what you say." Students verbally abuse cafeteria workers, staff personnel, teachers, and other students.

Have you ever experienced anything like the above examples? If so, you have experienced what could be referred to as a failure to understand and practice elements of civility. The question then arises whether we are less civil than we were at one time. Researchers Steve Farkas, Jean Johnson, Ann Duffett, and Kathleen Collins from the research organization Public Agenda attempted to answer this and other questions related to civility in a 2002 report, *Aggravating Circumstances: A Status Report on Rudeness in America.* They conducted a telephone survey of 2,013 adults 18 and over January 2-23, 2002. Here are some of the responses from their study:

- A lack of respect and courtesy is a serious problem for our society and we should try to address it. **—79% agree**

- They often or sometimes come across people who are rude and disrespectful. **—88% agree**

- Americans used to treat each other with more respect and courtesy in the past. **—73% agree**

- A major cause of rude and disrespectful behavior in our society is that too many parents are failing to teach respect to their kids. **—84% agree**

- 71% stated that when watching "...kids playing organized sports in the past year or so, they saw parents behaving inappropriately by yelling and screaming at coaches, referees or players."

This rudeness exists within our schools. In a study involving responses from 225 seniors in an urban public high school (Stephen B. Plank et. al., 2001), the authors determined that: 1) students are more often polite than rude toward teachers, but students also curse a lot; 2) students are more polite toward teachers than to each other and are much more likely to curse among fellow students than in the presence of teachers; 3) students describe themselves as capable of being either polite or crude; and 4) cursing at teachers depends upon the people and situation involved. They also noted:

> **Also, it is quite apparent** that the students in this study do not automatically grant respect or deference to teachers *qua* teachers. Rather, respect seems to be accorded to the person, not the position, by these students.... The data show that, all else being equal, students are more likely to curse at a teacher who is perceived as usually mean toward students as compared to a teacher who is perceived as usually nice. Also, students are more likely to curse at a teacher if they think they can get away with it rather than being disciplined. Perhaps related to this last point, and certainly relevant to school planning and organization, students are more likely to curse at a teacher if the student does not know them by name (p. 2).

These examples and the research indicate that a great number of us are not exercising daily the habits of civility essential for a community, state, or nation to flourish, rather than just survive. Let's look at the word *flourish*. According to the *New World Dictionary of the American Language* (1986), it is defined as "to blossom; to grow vigorously: succeed; thrive; prosper." We can survive with little variety in our diet and few cultural niceties to beautify our world and only a minimum of decorum or civil standards of conduct. But to *flourish*, we need to have our psychological needs met, such as having people love and care for us, and sharing practices that promote a civil and caring society. We flourish in a society that seeks common and just standards of conduct among its citizens, and we believe that schools should play a leading role in enabling children and adults to flourish. We can't emphasize enough that schools are essential transmitters of civil standards that promote or should promote a common good to insure the flourishing of its members.

Seeking a Common Good

This does not mean that everyone will always agree with the pursuit of a common good. There will be disagreement even about what *is* a common good. Sometimes the voices of a few individuals, such as Martin Luther King, Jr. or Nelson Mandela, raise the moral obligation for pursuit of a society's common good. The pursuit of a common good for our children and ourselves should involve a certain degree of sacrifice of individual impulses and desires in order to achieve a more loving and morally uplifting community and society for all. Without this pursuit, we condemn ourselves to relativism (judgment that is relative determined by events, personal preferences, choices, and feelings). Simply put, *we must strive to develop and then pass on the best of our moral and social ideology and practices and not assume children will figure it out on their own without instruction and modeling.*

The need for the schools and other institutions concerned with the moral and civil development of its citizens to step forward is arguably more pressing than in recent history. Yet as Alan Wolfe (2001) notes:

Compared to those who came before them, contemporary Americans cannot turn to the usual places in which moral authority was assumed to pass from generation to generation. Their churches tend to be absolutist in their teachings about moral truths. Their schools and universities have lost the confidence that they can recognize, let alone explain, something called reality. Members of their families care too much for personal satisfaction to accept the repression associated with classic ideas of renunciation and self-sacrifice. Were Americans to turn to institutions for instructions in moral guidance, they either would be unable to find them or would hear from them that they have little in the way of instruction to offer (p. 138).

Regrettably, within the scope of this work, we cannot address the role that families, faith communities, and other social organizations (e.g. scouting, 4-H, Rotary, Civitan) can and should play in promoting a common good. Our focus must be limited to the role schools can and must play in providing a crucial piece in forging a common good for us all. Whether we like it or not, schools, as institutions, are crucial for civilization and are essential for developing the moral and positive social attributes of children. The majority of children, unless they are home-schooled, spend six to nine hours a day, five days a week for 180-190 days a year in school. Now this does not mean that schools can or should take the place of parents. Parents are the first role models and social/moral educators, either good or bad, for their children, but due to the time children spend in school, it is imperative that the school community serve as positive social and moral educators and modelers of caring and kindness to all in the community. In other words, our job as educators is not just to teach the academics, but also to model for and incul- cate in children the moral and social sensibilities that will assist them in becoming social and moral contributors to their commu- nity. Only if we assert our obligation to teach civility and academics will we truly educate our children. Or as Theodore Roosevelt noted, "To educate a child in mind [and we would argue *civility*] and not morals is to educate a menace to society."

We must strive to develop and then pass on the best of our moral and social ideology and practices and not assume children will figure it out on their own without instruction and modeling.

What Schools Can Do

We believe that individuals, as well as groups, will flourish if 1) basic civilities are modeled, taught, and expected. This includes the development of basic civilities, which include good manners, caring, and showing respect for others; 2) individuals are taught an appreciation of larger philosophical ideas that focus on under- standing and promoting what is morally and socially desirable for all; and 3) individuals are given an opportunity to care about and contribute to the lives of others in their school and community. This book will focus on how we can establish a school climate that encourages civil growth among the adults and the children within the school. Let's go beyond the simple survival of schools—our goal is the flourishing of schools. Since we defined civility as cour- teous behavior or politeness, surely courtesy and politeness are essential elements of being civil, but by themselves, they are inad- equate. We can be polite toward others and still engage in inappropriate acts behind someone's back. A clear example for those of us old enough to remember is Eddie Haskell on "Leave it to Beaver." Eddie could charm the parents, but out of their sight, he was less than a moral model. You may have seen the same example in a teacher's lounge. A particular teacher is always a beacon of civility and caring around parents but is capable of rudeness and incivility toward students and her peers. A civil person is never without good manners, though an unethical person sometimes applies manners selectively to seek a particular advantage or influence. By themselves, manners are inadequate for civility to flourish; manners are necessary but are not sufficient to create the civil person, school, community, or nation.

What else might we need to promote civility? Civility must also reflect our literary and historical writings that through history have aimed at establishing and supporting a sense of moral truths and obligations, such as kindness, friendship, and love. For thousands of years, thinkers in philosophy, theology, literature, and the arts have attempted to formulate ideas and develop insights into understanding what our obligations are to those around us and to the human community as a whole. As educators, we must apply the wisdom found within the humanities to begin to develop little "philosophers" in our children. Where might we begin? Consider the maxims contained in the Golden Rule across cultures:

What you do not want done to yourself, do not do to others. **—Confucius**

We should behave to others as we wish others to behave to us. **—Aristotle**

What you hate, do not do to anyone. **—Judaism**

No one of you is a believer unless he loves for his brother what he loves for himself. **—Islam**

Do nothing to thy neighbor which thou wouldst not have him do to thee thereafter **—Hinduism**

Do unto others as you would have them do unto you. **—Christianity**

Hurt no others with that which pains thyself. **—Buddhism**

Cultures throughout the world have issued maxims on how we should treat others. Books and learned people have written, argued, and tried to apply these maxims. Plato, Aristotle, Kant, and other philosophers have struggled to determine a moral course of action that applies to everyone. Writers as diverse as Alice Walker, E.B. White, Shel Silverstein, Anne Frank, Dee Brown and George Orwell have illustrated the hardships and challenges that people struggle with as their moral insights develop. The way we assist children in developing their natural inquisitiveness concerning right and wrong, along with our obligations to others, will do much to help establish a civil climate in our school community.

In addition to using humanities to teach civility, consider the contributions of athletics and the sciences as well. Who cannot be moved by the humanity of a Jackie Robinson or an Albert Einstein? Teaching is primarily an intellectual pursuit and yet, its companion, the development of good manners or habits of civility, allows this intellectual pursuit to develop and flourish. It is hard to engage in demanding intellectual pursuits unless there is a civil climate that encourages the exchange of ideas. Unless we are civil *to* each other we will not learn *from* each other. Therefore, civility will demand our intellectual efforts, as well as our manners.

We must also consider how our service to children and adults in our schools and community sends a message concerning an obligation to care for and serve others in building the civil society. It is not enough to be polite or merely understand the importance of kindness and caring toward others. We must show it in our actions! We as the adults, as well as the students, must serve each other and create opportunities for kindness and caring to grow within our community. Since good manners are based on respect, they are the starting point for teaching kindness and caring for others. However, civility is also exhibited by the child who readily assists a handicapped child, as well as the handicapped child who assists another. The larger concept of civility that we are promoting encompasses caring for others—in our classrooms, our work places, our neighborhoods, and our nation—and calls for putting hearts and hands into the action. We care and serve each other not to satisfy an academic requirement, but to help ourselves love and be loved by others. Losing the "me" and considering the needs of "you" is a cat-

We as the adults, as well as the students, must serve each other and create opportunities for kindness and caring to grow within our community.

alyst in the development of a person capable of love for others, as well as a citizen who works to create the civil society.

So, our understanding of civility—which goes well beyond the dictionary definition—must involve 1) the development of good manners and habits that promote good behavior; 2) an intellectual focus on the moral and social obligations to create a civil society; and 3) actions of love and caring that are developed through service directed toward the needs of others. These three practices testify to an understanding of the requirements of the civil school, the civil student, and civil educator. In essence, a civil school is one that practices "knowing the good, loving the good, and doing the good" (phrasing that was first expressed by Dr. Kevin Ryan and Dr. Thomas Lickona) to distill the concepts we have explained here. Achieving a civil school, in which all three of the elements are fully active, will require the development of *virtue* in ourselves as well as our students. Ryan and Karen E. Bohlin (1999) define virtue as:

The word *virtue* comes from the Latin *vir*, which has a root meaning of "force" or "agency." In Latin the expression *virtus moralis* became the established equivalent of the Greek expression *arete ethike*, "moral virtue" or "character excellence." The Greek word *arete* means "excellence." ...Virtue is both the disposition to think, feel, and act in morally excellent ways, and the exercise of this disposition. Furthermore, it serves as both a means and an end of human happiness. As a means, virtues are those habits and dispositions that enable us to live out our responsibilities more gracefully (p. 44-45).

Do we not admire those who think, feel, and act in morally excellent ways? Think of the teacher who made the biggest difference in your life. You may not remember all this teacher taught you, but you surely remember how this teacher lived his/her life in your presence. You recognize and admire the virtue in this person. Developing virtue in ourselves so we can be a beacon of light to our students requires that we develop and model the intellectual and social habits that promote excellence. Let us now consider how we can gain a better understanding of how we can achieve this and assist others in their pursuit.

Macro and Micro Requirements

The development of "those habits and dispositions" that are found within a virtuous person also are found in the civil person. Respect, responsibility for one's actions, and acts of kindness toward friends and strangers are the hallmarks of a civil person and ultimately, a civil society. This individual is further moved by ideas and wisdom learned and internalized through study of the humanities. In this manner, a person will need manners, but also aptitudes to explore and act upon the requirements needed to promote a civil climate. Perhaps one way of analyzing this issue is to recognize that there are different layers of morality or virtue. James Rest, et. al. (1999) note:

> **Just as in the field of economics** a distinction is made between macroeconomics and microeconomics, so also it is useful to distinguish levels of phenomena in "macromorality" and "micromorality." Macromorality concerns the formal structures of society that are involved in making cooperation possible in a society level (in which not just kin, friends, and long-known acquaintances are interrelated, but strangers, competitors, and diverse class, ethnic groups, and religions are as well). Examples of the special concerns of macromorality include the rights and responsibilities of free speech, due-process rights of the accused, nondiscriminatory work practices, freedom of religion, and equity in economic and educational opportunity.
>
> On the other hand, micromorality concerns developing relationships with particular others, and with an individual's creating consistent virtues within him or herself throughout everyday life. Examples of micromorality include displaying courtesy and helpfulness to those with whom one personally interacts; caring in intimate relationships; observing birthdays and other personal events of friends and family; being courteous while driving a car; being punctual for appointments; and generally acting in a decent, responsible, empathic way in one's dealings with others (p. 2).

Our move toward civility must recognize both the *macro* and *micro* requirements of being a moral or civil person. The macro view of morality/civility gives us our philosophical precepts, our moral standards, in developing a just society. Our macromorality is based upon thousands of years of philosophical and religious thought, writings, and application. Based upon this tradition, we seek to prescribe a best course of action to promote flourishing among all constituents, whether we are personally connected to those other individuals or not. What we regard as civil within a macro-moral tradition might change, but it is incremental and generally, at least in the West, it is oriented toward the establishment of more and better rights and freedoms—hopefully with responsibility in the application of these rights. We have also seen, through history, the development of the idea that our obligations to others extend far beyond our immediate family and even our country. It now demands acts of caring on a worldwide basis to those we never know or see. Thus, although the importance of specific macro- and micromoral practices and requirements may change more swiftly at the micromorality level, the demands for applying standards that promote individual and group flourishing continues: *We should treat others as we want to be treated.*

The micro view of morality/civility requires that we develop habits of civility which lead to a fair standard of how people are treated in our day-to-day activities. We can acknowledge that good manners are aspects of a civil person and that these manners are based upon social expectations. We will always be expected to thank a person who gives us a gift, or to speak respectfully to our peers and superiors at work. We are also expected to apologize when wrong, and forgive when asked.

Influence of Popular Culture

This is not easy, but it is very important. We must, if possible, try to reach a consensus and standard of civility that will promote flourishing for our children as well as adults. This civil ideal is in stark contrast to what many of our children are being exposed to. We and our children are being bombarded with messages and images that promote the self to the detriment of the community. Watch television. Play video games. Look at product advertising. Listen to professional athletes. Many of their messages, as well as those in the lyrics of some teen-popular songs, promote incivility and disrespect. Individual freedom is paramount. Women are denigrated. Sex is a right or a good recreational activity. Cursing can be directed at anyone one chooses. Violence is a natural part of life. This lack of civility is not just heard or seen in the streets of our communities. It also comes to us consistently via the media within our homes.

The idea of violence as a normal part of television programming is apparent to anyone who sits down for an evening of television viewing. After examining more than 10,000 hours of TV

> *We must try to reach a consensus and standard of civility that will promote flourishing for our children as well as adults.*

programming between 1994 and 1997, the National Television Violence Study (cited by Schlozman, 2003) concluded that young people view about 10,000 acts of violence per year with more than half of all TV programs having violent content. The study also determined that 38% of violence is committed by so-called "attractive perpetrators." These are individuals who look fine and perhaps dress well. In addition, more than half of the perpetrators of violence act without either pain or remorse. The question arises as to whether violence on television influences behavior of children and ultimately adults. In 2001, Surgeon General of the United States David Satcher released a comprehensive report, *Youth Violence: A Report of the Surgeon General*, which attempted to assess youth violence and the causal relationships between violence and various environmental inputs, including television. In utilizing longitudinal studies which attempted to assess whether exposure to media violence in early childhood can be related to later aggression and violence, the Surgeon General concluded that:

> **...these longitudinal studies** show a small, but often statistically significant, long-term relationship between viewing television violence in childhood and later aggression, especially in late adolescence and early adulthood. Some evidence suggests that more aggressive children watch more violence, but the evidence is stronger that watching media violence is a precursor of increased aggression (appendix 4-B p. 5 of downloaded report).

The Surgeon General's report also examined the influence of music videos. He concluded that, "Randomized experiments indicate that exposure to violent or antisocial rap videos can increase aggressive thinking, but no research has yet tested how such exposure directly affects physical aggression." (appendix 4-B p.6 of downloaded report) Based on the Surgeon General's report, we may conclude that the media is having some negative influences on our children.

Moving beyond the violence and its impact found within the media, we must also acknowledge that too many of our children are growing up without emotional and basic economic security in the home. Developing habits of civility are especially difficult with children from homes or communities that are struggling to define and model these civilities for their children. Recently, a director of a preschool program working with "at-risk" children stated to one of the authors that unless we can model and develop in these children habits of civility and kindness toward others, the task of teaching them to read in the schools will be far more difficult. She added that children without emotional security and good modeling in their homes will require far greater training and effort on the part of the educators in developing habits of civility before these children can focus on the academics.

This can apply to a neighborhood and it can also apply to a school. In far too many schools—in inner cities as well as affluent suburbs—a lack of civility in students who haven't been taught basic civilities is a major influence on the climate of the school. This affects teachers and other students and the problem compounds as students observe uncivil behavior and see that no consequences ensue. In fact, the primary consequences may be that more and more teachers are leaving the profession, particularly in high social and economic-need schools.

It is Different Now

Edwin Delattre (2000), Dean of the School of Education at Boston University recognizes the difficulty faced by teachers:

Often, some or many of the students they are expected to teach come to school ill-prepared, ill-mannered, undisciplined, inconsiderate, self-indulgent, lazy, misogynistic, vulgar, obscene, dishonest, brutal, predatory, or violent either by initiative or by reaction to the contrived or imagined slight. Some students bring with them to school what Charles Murray calls "the ethics of male adolescents who haven't been taught any better." I would add that some of these students are females, and that some boys and girls, children and youths, in school today live their lives outside of school in conditions vividly pictured by Hogarth. Even supposedly advantaged children are coarsened by neglectful parents who leave them to their own devices in endless exposure to the vulgarity of popular culture as purveyed in the crude humor of the typical sitcom.

Many teachers must greet such students day after day—and must do so without benefit of administrators who have the knowledge and the courage to establish and maintain basic standards of discipline, conduct, safety, and civility in the schools for which they are responsible. Parents and members of advocacy groups can also be unbelievably nasty to teachers—and with impunity, where administrators are craven (p. 160).

He continues:

When civility becomes a sensitivity that, like indiscriminate tolerance, casts aside regard for the truth, it bears little resemblance to civility understood as liberal learning, manners and morals, behavior appropriate to the discourse of civilized people, or even plain courtesy. Indeed, where the idea of civility is equated or conjoined with the idea of sensitively coddling sensitivities that make us too frail to bear the truth, civility cannot any further be associated with our having any sort of genuine and decent respect for one another (pp. 164-65).

One of the authors, when speaking with groups of educators, generally asks how many of them cursed or verbally abused their teachers during their K-12 years. Rarely are hands raised, although occasionally someone states that he or she heard another child verbally abuse a teacher. The next question gets far more positive responses: "How many of you *thought* about cussing out a teacher?" Lots of hands go up at this because it's a far different question. Many of us considered what we wanted to say, but we *didn't* say it. We knew this was wrong. Besides, for many of us, the consequences at home if our parents heard about us disrespecting a teacher would have been rather severe. Although we can offer no scientific proof, after talking to thousands of educators, we feel comfortable

stating that there has definitely been an increase in our schools of foul language and other disrespectful verbal exchanges from student to teacher and teacher to student and the subsequent behavior that grows from this lack of courtesy. Why is this so? Wasn't this unacceptable in years past? Wasn't this considered inappropriate? Why did we, as educators and community members, allow this to occur?

An explanation of this would demand far more than the scope of this book. Yet we can consider briefly several trends which may explain why we will need to work hard to restore a common standard of civility within the school. Francis Fukuyama (1999) notes:

Since the 1960's, the West has experienced a series of liberation movements that have sought to free individuals from the constraints of traditional social norms and moral rules.... Pop psychology, from the human-potential movement of the 1960's to the self-esteem trend of the 1980's, sought to free individuals from stifling social expectations....

As people soon discovered, there are serious problems with a culture of unbridled individualism, in which the breaking of rules becomes, in a sense, the only remaining rule. The first has to do with the fact that moral values and social rules are not simply arbitrary constraints on individual choice but the precondition for any kind of cooperative enterprise. Indeed social scientists have recently begun to refer to a society's stock of shared values as "social capital."...Social virtues such as honesty, reciprocity, and the keeping of commitments are not worthwhile just as ethical values; they also have a tangible dollar value and help the groups that practice them to achieve shared ends.

The second problem with a culture of individualism is that it ends up being bereft of community. A community is not formed every time a group of people happen to interact with one another; true communities are bound together by the values, norms, and experiences their members share. The deeper and more strongly held those common values, the stronger the sense of community....

A society dedicated to the constant upending of norms and rules in the name of expanding individual freedom of choice will find itself increasingly disorganized, atomized, isolated, and incapable of carrying out common goals and tasks. The same society that wants no limits on its technological innovation also sees no limits on many forms of personal behavior and the consequence is a rise in crime, broken families, parents' failure to fulfill obligations to children, neighbors' refusal to take responsibility for one another, and citizens' opting out of public life (pp. 59-60).

> The loss of our shared "social capital" has profound effects on our community and ultimately, our schools. Unless we can develop a common understanding of the norms and standards that communities and schools should model and teach to their children, we will continue to stand on shifting sands rather than the firm foundation that a civil and just community must have. The norms are further violated when we lose a sense of community because of the demands of work on us within an increasingly hectic modern life. More time spent at work results in less time for community involvement. Robert Putnam, in *Bowling Alone: The Collapse and Revival of American Community* (2000) illustrated that

time spent commuting to and from work in an ever-increasing amount of time in traffic leads to a reduction in civic involvement. What school has enough parent volunteers or attendees at PTO/PTA meetings? What religious institution has enough individuals to fill the committees as well as participate in its missions? How much time do we spend working or even socializing with our neighbors? Charles Taylor, in *The Ethics of Authenticity* (1997) notes that the demands of our modern society has changed us. Hundreds of years ago, one would spend most of one's labor and life around a group in a village or community. We knew each other. We depended on each other. Now many of us spend much of our time on the move from one job to another throughout the nation and the world. Even if we are located in a general area, many people spend their sleeping hours in a suburb and then rise early in the morning for a long commute to a centralized work area where we may have few of our suburban neighbors as workmates. Taylor notes that our modern world far too often celebrates and centers fulfillment on the individual who "...tends to see fulfillment as just of the self, neglecting or delegitimizing the demands that come from beyond our own desires or aspirations, be they from history, tradition, society, nature, or God: they foster; in other words, a radical anthropocentrism [considering man as the central fact, or final aim of the universe] (p.58). Taylor continues:

> **From its very inception, this kind of society** has involved mobility, at first of peasants off the land and to cities, and then across oceans and continents to new countries, and finally, today, from city to city following employment opportunities. Mobility is in a sense forced on us. Old ties are broken down, At the same time, city dwelling is transformed by the immense concentrations of population of the modern metropolis. By its very nature, this involves much more impersonal and casual contact, in place of the more intense face-to-face relations in earlier times. All this cannot but generate a culture in which the outlook of social atomism becomes more and more entrenched (p. 59).

The increase in social atomism, or seeing oneself as separate and not connected with the wants and needs of others in our home, community, or nation, recognizes that more and more individuals see themselves as distinct from the community and society around them. Many individuals only go to work and then go home to the television. Without community involvement—spending social time and bettering relationships with others within the home and community—it is far too easy to focus just on *my* needs or *my* wants and less on the civil demands of a community. Life becomes focused on my rights in the community, not my responsibilities to the community (e.g., I have a right to keep junky cars on the street and I will do so. I like to have loud parties so I will continue this, even though there are children and others who may not want or need to hear the noise.). Being responsible requires relationships with others; it is the recognition that my wants must be tempered by the needs of others. An over-focused sense on my rights without a concept of responsibility results in what Walter Percy called "the suck of self." This plays out in schools as some educators work just for a paycheck, doing only the bare minimum with the curriculum, without considering the moral and social implications of their actions. They are modeling behavior that their students will emulate—imagine a world in which everyone does only the bare minimum. Some parents may and do come to the school demanding special privileges for their children without considering the needs of the total school community. For example, in Chapel Hill, North Carolina, a parent wrote to the school system with the alert that their preschooler was highly allergic to peanuts and they had three years to get peanuts entirely out of the school lunch program. What about the desire of other parents to have their children eat peanut butter sandwiches separate from the child? What about other strategies the parents could suggest so that the needs of others could be taken into account? What about some common dialogue on how the problem might be solved instead of issuing edicts? Educators sometimes see children focus just on their needs or wants without consideration of the needs of their classmates. Some children may seek to isolate particular children from their group just because they can. Students bully children for money or to humiliate them. One parent told one of the authors that her son would not clean up the class table in the lunchroom since this was *not* the job of her child. Taylor refers to this as the individualism of self-fulfillment:

> **This individualism involves a centering** on the self and a concomitant shutting out, or even unawareness, of the greater issues or concerns that transcend the self, be they religious, political, historical. As a consequence, life is narrowed or flattened (p. 14).

If my focus is on "me" and not "we," then meeting my needs is of paramount importance, at least to me. I do not seek moral principles or historical or religious precepts to justify my actions. Ryan and Bohlin (1999) note:

> **In the world of personal relativism,** the individual is king. Although she may choose to obey the law as her only moral norm, whatever else she does is a matter of personal choice. And if a person should choose to break the law, what matters most is that she doesn't get caught. Morality becomes a purely personal matter. The only moral standard that remains is that there are no absolute moral standards or norms. There are just individual values. Confronted with an ethical problem, we are responsible for solving it only in the way that suits us best. We are our own private judge and jury (p. 36).

Have we not seen this attitude in our schools among some students, adults, or parents? A coach decides to break the rules regarding grades and attendance of particular players for athletics because he needs to have a winning team. A teacher decides that she does not like team planning in the middle school so she boycotts team meetings. A child refuses to follow the rules of a class because he is accustomed to having his way and does not like the new rules. The focus on "me" leaves little time to consider the needs of others. And without considering the needs of others, our schools lose community. This is critical. We believe it is not a demand for greater academic standards such as No Child Left Behind or any mandated curricular evaluation program that is creating stress and incivility within the schools. *Our rising levels of stress and incivility result from the demand for academic standards in an environment that has lost the expectation of civil standards that we should live by and teach to others.*

What are our civil standards? What are our limits and expectations we have of our students and ourselves? What are our moral and social obligations toward others and ourselves? Is everyone on the same page? Are we consistent? Do the needs of "me" trump the needs of the group? All of these questions deserve serious attention. But ultimately, we believe that a school will not achieve its academic standards unless it first achieves civil standards. To achieve civil standards, we must forge a climate that models caring and kindness with rights and responsibilities. In some ways it is a dance, one that we must learn to do well. Simply put, if students and teachers are more civil to each other and if we focus on promoting a sense of caring and fairness for all, the members of the school will have a greater opportunity to meet their academic and civil standards of a just and caring community.

Turning Back to Face the Future

In far too many schools, we have a social upheaval that increasingly threatens the norms of civil life within our schools. Indeed,

some schools are hanging onto a civil environment by a thread. Personal relativism or the right of an individual or a small group of people to determine what is right/wrong or appropriate/inappropriate in our schools, without the consideration of the social and moral needs of the larger group, may have a serious effect on the school life of students and teachers. This is even more apparent if we, as educators, are confused about the norms and standards of civility we wish to model and teach to our children. We must reestablish a norm of civility, which will demand far more than manners. A civil school must have manners of appropriate behavior but it must also have kindness, caring, and a healthy interchange of ideas that a democracy demands. We must go beyond personal relativism in the moral domain and reach for common standards. From the establishment of common standards, we must assume a philosophical position that will guide us in adopting these standards in our own lives and inculcating them in those we teach. To do this, we must visit ancient Greece.

If we assume that reestablishing or enhancing a civil climate in our schools is a desirable goal, we must first determine what we, as educators, can do to mentor and develop in students the practice of civility toward others. Let's consider the ideas and insights of perhaps the greatest philosopher of all time—Aristotle. Before addressing his important insights, let us first consider the question raised by Aristotle's teacher, Plato. In a dialogue involving his teacher, Socrates, and Socrates' student, Meno, Plato asks the question of how virtue is acquired.

Can you tell me, Socrates—can virtue be taught, or is it rather to be acquired by practice? Or is it neither to be practiced nor to be learned but something that comes to men by nature or in some other way? (*Meno* 70a)

With this, Plato asked the question that we are still, today, trying to answer: "How does one become a good person?" Does one become good through the development of good habits via practice? Does one learn to be good via dialogue and conversation? Is goodness innate? Is it a combination of all three? Two out of three? These are not simple questions. Each one demands clear thinking and dialogue to tentatively forge an answer. Although Plato proposed the question, our initial efforts will focus on how Aristotle addressed this issue. Through him, we can gain a greater understanding of what we must do to create the civil school. First we will note what is needed to raise the good child.

In the last chapter of the *Nicomachean Ethics*, Aristotle attempts to answer Meno's question. He advances an explanation (1179b4-31) concerning why it is that only someone with a good upbringing, by which he meant having good habits and a kind disposition toward others, can benefit from the kind of argument and intellectual discussion contained in his lectures. He begins by questioning whether we are good by nature or whether we become good by arguments or discussions. He then determines that the development of good habits is the foundation for future debate and discussions on living the good/civil life. Aristotle writes:

Plato asked the question that we are still, today, trying to answer: "How does one become a good person?"

Now some think that we are made good by nature, others by habituation, others by teaching. Nature's part evidently does not depend on us, but as a result of some divine causes, is present in those who are truly fortunate; while argument and teaching, we may suspect, are not powerful with all men, but the soul of the student must first have been cultivated, by means of habits, for noble joy and noble hatred, like earth which is to nourish the seed. For he who lives as passion directs will not hear argument that dissuades him, nor understand it if he does; and how can we persuade one in such a state to change his ways? And in general passion seems to yield not to argument, but to force. The character, then, must somehow be there already with a kinship to virtue, loving what is noble and hating what is base (Burnyeat, p. 75).

According to Aristotle, before one can cognitively appreciate what is noble, one must have developed a noble character. How does this occur? It evolves in children who have seen others model it and who have, through their own practice and efforts, developed good habits. They have learned what is noble 1) by practicing what is noble, and 2) through the work of a good teacher or parent who recognizes the emerging developmental intellectual abilities of the child and helps the child establish and value the practices of civility that lead to noble character.

For a moment let us separate the practice from the reflection (although in reality this is probably impossible because the human mind is always processing experience. It's important to note that we don't develop or practice habits without some cognitive activity!). Let us assume that we value and model politeness in our classrooms. We value verbal civility, such as commonly saying "please," "thank you," and "excuse me," as well as respectful practices such as holding the door for those walking behind us, helping those who need assistance, taking correct seats in a timely way, passing papers forward quietly, raising hands to be recognized so as not to interrupt others. Those of us who want that behavior in our classrooms model, work with students, and have them practice this over and over. Perhaps we have asked students to define what *respect* means and what it looks like in practice. Maybe the students have given some examples like those noted above. Through modeling, intent, and practice, we work hard to turn these ideals into habits, which are regularly practiced, praised, and valued.

Even as students are practicing the habits, they are reflecting on what they are doing—perhaps immaturely at first, but as they get older, they're capable of much higher levels of thought. We can facilitate this consciously, choosing to adopt civil practices. For example, at the elementary school level, we can schedule a morning meeting to discuss these practices. We can talk with students about how we feel when we're treated kindly. At the middle school or high school level, we can study George Washington's famous practices/maxims of civility and discuss how we can apply these maxims to our own life. Perhaps we could hold a classroom seminar addressing the issue of civility as Washington perceived it. Students can work cooperatively to solve a school or classroom problem regarding an issue of fairness. Opportunities for caring for and serving others in the school and community could be discussed. These are only a few of the ways in which we are now building cognitive awareness upon the habits of civility that have developed through modeling and practice. Reflection will play a role in our efforts. However, we must remember that it is much easier to teach a child about the importance of civility and kindness toward others *after* a child has developed the habits of civility and kindness. Christina Hoff Sommers in *The War Against Boys* (2000) notes:

We value verbal civility as well as respectful practices.

> **Habituation to right behavior** comes before an appreciation or understanding of why we should be good. First, children must be socialized by inculcating into them habits of decency and using suitable punishments and rewards to discipline them to behave well. Eventually they will understand the reasons for and advantages of being moral human beings (p. 189).

More about moral practices and the use of the curriculum to promote a civil school will be discussed in later chapters. The key factor is that good habit formation and intellectual development are necessary to create the civil school.

The continuous development of civil habits represents the foundation or predecessor for reflection. Aristotle calls the predecessor of ethical reflection "the that."

We already know that in ethics good habits are a prerequisite for grasping "the that." It is now added that habituation is actually a way of grasping it, on a par with, though different from, induction, perception, and other modes of acquisition which Aristotle does not specify (the ancient commentators fill out the list for him by mentioning intellectual intuition and experience). Each kind of starting point comes with a mode of acquisition appropriated to it; to give a couple of examples from the ancient commentators, we learn by induction that all men breathe, by perception that fire is hot. In ethics the appropriate mode for at least some starting point is habituation... (Burnyeat p. 75).

"The that" is the starting point for the habits that mold the character of a child. From these habits a child is better able, as he or she intellectually matures, to appreciate teaching and learning about the rationale concerning what is noble or just. Consider this from a teacher's perspective. You can possess the greatest curriculum in the world, but if the climate of the school does not produce civility, then the excellence of the curriculum will never achieve its promise. The climate is the precursor to successful learning of the curriculum; or as Dr. Kevin Ryan notes concerning the importance of character education, "Character development is not another thing on a teacher's plate, it *is* the plate."

The same applies to our present focus. Civility is not another piece to be added onto the plate of an educator, it *is* the plate upon which all else is placed. Aristotle refers to the arguments or reasoned inquiry as being inadequate to stimulate goodness among youth unless these youth are "true lovers of what is noble and hating what is base." If they have not developed the habits of goodness, words to persuade them to do so will fail to achieve their goals. Wisdom from adults and from peers is more easily received by those who have developed habits of civility. The developed habits create the reference point to better receive, understand, and apply the teachings. Simply put, the development of the intellect in fostering moral action or civility is necessary but it is not sufficient to develop the good child. "The that," which is the precursor or at least the base of intellectual efforts, is essential in developing the civil child and hopefully, the civil school.

R.S. Peters has noted: "The palace of wisdom has to be entered through by the courtyard of habit" (p. 314). We couldn't agree more. Aristotle recognized that no amount of reasoning or quality arguments of doing the good will change a person who has not "tasted" or practiced what is noble. Perhaps a better way of stating this is to recognize that excellent efforts toward shaping the intellect of the child will fall far short unless one first works to shape the habits of civility within the self as well as the child.

This is what we must address. We, as educators, must focus on how we model and inculcate in children a genuine and demonstrable respect for one another. To do this, we must make the development of virtue and character in children, which leads to a perspective of one as a civil being, as important as the academics in our schools. Our efforts in this primer will focus on how we can bring civility back or enhance the civility within schools. We realize that this is a difficult topic and one that far too many schools have been reluctant to bridge. However, the people of a school must bridge it. It is imperative to bring civility back to schools to insure a climate that will allow learning to occur and "flourishing" to begin or grow.

You can possess the greatest curriculum in the world, but if the climate of the school does not produce civility, then the excellence of the curriculum will never achieve its promise.

To succeed in our efforts we must first recognize basic practices that if applied would promote a civil environment. We have borrowed Stephen L. Carter's principles of civility found in his book *Civility: Manners, Morals, and Etiquette of Democracy* (1998) to guide us in our pursuit of the civil school. His ideas will be integrated in our efforts. Below are fifteen of his principles. Please take some time to consider how these principles could be applied and developed within your school.

1. Our duty to be civil toward others does not depend on whether we like them or not.

2. Civility requires that we sacrifice for strangers, not just for people we happen to know.

3. Civility has two parts: generosity, even when it is costly, and trust, even when there is risk.

4. Civility creates not merely a negative duty not to do harm, but an affirmative duty to do good.

5. Civility requires a commitment to live a common moral life, so we should try to follow the norms of the community if the norms are not actually immoral.

6. We must come into the presence of our fellow human beings with a sense of awe and gratitude.

7. Civility assumes that we will disagree; it requires us not to mask our differences but to resolve them respectfully.

8. Civility requires that we listen to others with knowledge of the possibility that they are right and we are wrong.

9. Civility requires that we express ourselves in ways that demonstrate our respect for others.

10. Civility requires resistance to the dominance of social life by the values of the marketplace. Thus, the basic principles of civility—generosity and trust—should apply as fully in the market and in politics as in every other human activity.

11. Civility allows criticism of others, and sometimes even requires it, but the criticism should always be civil.

12. Civility discourages the use of legislation rather than conversation to settle disputes, except as a last, carefully considered resort.

13. Teaching civility, by word and example, is an obligation of the family. The state must not interfere with the family's effort to create a coherent moral universe for its children.

14. Civility values diversity, disagreement, and the possibility of resistance, and therefore the state must not use education to try to standardize our children.

15. Religions do their greatest service to civility when they preach not only love of neighbor but resistance to wrong (pp. 279-285).

Carter's notions of civility demand something of us, and that is *sacrifice*. We have to sacrifice our individual impulses or desires in order to consider the needs of others. My life and actions must recognize the needs of others. This acknowledgment and the actions that are required are the beginning of a civil community. This is the way we encourage flourishing of the individual as well as the group. This is the thrust of civility, but it is not an easy task. A nation that prides itself on individual freedom cannot long continue unless there is recognition that with freedom come responsibilities and obligations to others, and herein lies the tension. Tension exists between my rights and desires and the requirement to sacrifice some of my wants for the needs of the community. To have a civil school, we must recognize individual needs and wants (in order that individual students can develop their intellectual passions) and also recognize the needs of the community. Sacrifice of some desires or impulses (e.g., my "right" to yell at someone who insults me, or my impulse to ridicule someone who is different) is essential for a civil school. We must work to supplant impulses with habit and intellect that is focused on respect, responsibility and caring about each other and the greater community.

In conclusion, we need social communion and must establish mores or standards that act as a guide to help us as we help our students mature from children to adults. The school must either support or be the chief architect for some children in developing a notion of civility toward others. The remainder of this book will define how we believe this can be achieved.

We have to sacrifice our individual impulses or desires in order to consider the needs of others.

CHAPTER 2

Rethinking Childhood: Tapping the Civility Potential

What the best and wisest parent wants for his own child, that must be what the community wants for all its children. Any other ideal for our schools is narrow and unlovely; acted upon, it destroys our democracy.

—John Dewey, *School and Society* (1910)

Being civil toward others is desirable for all within a culture and, for our purposes, within a school. It demonstrates the respect we all wish to receive, and it encourages better communication on all issues at all levels. So, how do we get to that point? Ideally, every child would be taught at home how to be civil and respectful of others, but we know that is not the case. We believe it is incumbent upon the schools to encourage students to adopt civility and kindness toward others. We cannot empower children to act and think with kindness and civility unless the children, as well as the adults, within the school model and develop consistent practices toward developing the habits of civil behavior. Let us emphasize that we are not born with an understanding of what civility is. However, we may be programmed at birth with the potential to develop good habits of caring and concern that can result in us becoming beacons of civility. William Damon, in his work *Greater Expectations* (1995), writes:

The seeds of the moral sense are sown at conception, and its roots are firmly established at birth. Every infant enters this world prepared to respond socially, and in a moral manner, to others. Every child has the capacity to acquire moral character. The necessary emotional response systems, budding cognitive awareness, and personal dispositions are there from the start. Although, unfortunately, not every child grows into a responsible and caring person, the potential to do so is native to every member of the species (p. 132).

Are We Born With Enough?

Damon's premise is that the "wiring" is in place for the development of good moral citizens before children are born. As any observant adult recognizes, children from a very early age are constantly observing their world, seeking to understand the process and order in it. They want to find fairness and goodness, first for themselves and then, as they get older, for others. They want to solve problems and are capable of doing this. Killen (1991) noted that children are capable of solving 70% of their disputes during free play using reconciliation by the instigator or through compromising and bargaining. This is done *without* the intervention of the teacher. With their quick aptitude for learning and natural openness, they can very willingly adopt the practices and, we hope, the attitudes that yield highly civil individuals. Yet merely having the "wiring" doesn't guarantee that a child will develop into a good citizen. Having the capability does not guarantee development of moral character. Much depends on what we, as the adults, do to assist the child in developing the capacities with which he is born.

Building on extensive research, Damon argues that there are four overlapping processes present at birth that facilitate ethical awareness:

- Moral emotions, such as empathy, fear and guilt
- Moral judgment to determine conduct in matters of justice, caring, truthfulness, responsibility, and ethical duty
- Social cognition to relate to the social world
- Self-understanding to glean awareness of our past, present, and future self and to master self-control (p. 133)

To allow these processes to reach fruition in the child, we must instruct, model, and allow time for the child to learn, practice, and expand social and intellectual habits that contribute to the moral and social development of children. This will require adults acting as role models to children, as well as adults providing a rich learning/caring environment. If we want our students to use polite language to each other, we must show them how to do it. We must use polite language to them and to other adults, and we must require them to use polite language when speaking to adults and to others in their peer group. Developing habits of civility is one way we build upon the inborn processes that are present at birth. This is how we add some "current" to the wiring of our children.

Another strategy to develop civil practices in students at a deeper level is to encourage them to reflect, analyze, and discuss readings, sports, arts, and other intellectual fare that addresses the issue of civility toward others. A teacher can lead a discussion of news items about road rage, unsportsmanlike behavior, or a civic speaker being jeered. These topics also make excellent essay assignments. We ourselves must engage often in these discussions to keep our intellect and positions ready for students' questions. (More on the intellectual practice of civility will follow in a later chapter.) Through education and modeling in family as well as school life, we socialize and assist children in their march toward adulthood. It's not hard, especially with young children, to make a good or bad impression, because young children look up to adults and want to be like them. Who hasn't seen a child seeking to emulate the actions of a parent, i.e., shaving or cooking? Even when children seem not to notice, they are paying very close attention to our words and actions. Sometimes children point out the smallest inconsistencies between what we say one ought to do and what we actually do. What parent hasn't had that happen?

The truth, or a grievous inconsistency, pointed out by a child can cause a parent or teacher much chagrin at times. One of the authors was driving once with his three-year-old daughter when a car pulled out in front of them, nearly causing an accident. Without thinking, Dad blurted out a choice line of words. Several weeks later, the father and daughter had another near-accident. This time, he didn't need to say the words; his daughter did! She

If we want our students to use polite language to each other, we must show them how to do it.

copied perfectly what she had heard, both the phrasing and the application. Now, many years later, that daughter uses very appropriate language to express her concerns, and her father is working hard to achieve the same. Older children are watching us even

Children young and old are always paying close attention to what we say, what we do, and how well they match.

more closely. Have you ever worn some new clothes to school or had your hair done in a different manner? Perhaps no one at home commented on the difference, but how many children at school noticed the new clothes or the new look? This occurs whether one is in elementary or high school. As children mature, peer groups have a greater influence over their ideas and actions. Still, adults who are meaningfully involved with children have profound impacts on their social and intellectual attitudes and actions. Children young and old are always paying close attention to what we say, what we do, and how well they match. With that kind of attention, it's an excellent opportunity to *show* them how good, caring people behave toward others.

To Rousseau or Not to Rousseau

We feel there is a great need for adults to deliberately model and have our children consider, practice, and develop the habits of kindness and caring. However, not everyone believes that we should, with intent and consistency, work to "socialize" children by modeling and teaching them appropriate behavior. The 18th-century French philosopher Jean-Jacques Rousseau maintained that children should be children before they become adults. He believed that children have their own unique ways of thinking and feeling. In his work, *Emile* (1762), Rousseau argued passionately for a rethinking of childhood education. He maintained that children should not be contaminated by the world. Rousseau believed that man's original nature was good and that society had corrupted this good. This concept of original nature has some connection to Damon's concept of innate traits such as moral emotion, judgment, social cognition, and self-understanding. However, Damon would acknowledge that children need *nurturing* at an early age by those committed to the development of these processes. Rousseau's argument dismissed the importance of the adult, at least through adolescence. For Rousseau, in order to provide the best possible rearing of the child, it was necessary to raise the child up in the country without the influence the child would have in a city. If by nature we are born good, then a retreat back to nature will allow this goodness to flourish and for the child to grow in accordance with his/her nature: "Nature wants children to be children before being men." He maintained that, left to their own accord, children will develop into morally sensitive individuals through their intuitions, experiences, and feelings. Rousseau felt there were five stages of development from birth to adulthood. We will briefly examine stages two and three which, cover ages 2-15. Rousseau's position to avoid having children contaminated by the world of adult ideas and sensibilities was most evident in stage 2 (age 2-12) of Emile's development. Rousseau felt there should be *no* direct moral instruction or verbal learning (i.e., classroom activities) during this time. The child should interact more with things and objects through his senses and not as much with adults or the intellectual ideas of adults. This trend continues into preadolescence, stage 3 (age 12-15), when Rousseau felt the child should not be exposed to ideas that are beyond his immediate comprehension. The only book the child would be allowed to read would be *Robinson Crusoe*, a story about a self-sufficient and solitary man. After the age of 15, the child begins to recognize a larger world and begins to develop an interest in the social, and eventually, the moral calling of adulthood. As the child then continues to mature toward adulthood, more academic teaching and preparation for life as a member of society should occur. We cannot discount Rousseau entirely. He correctly gleaned that there are stages of development. The child grows into adulthood, he is not born a little adult. He also recognized that a child's brain is different from adults and has different abilities and sensibilities at different stages of development. We can value Rousseau's insights and the role that intuition, experience, and feelings play in the development of the child, but they are not enough to insure the development of the good, morally developed child. What type of modeling and instruction are the children experiencing when left to their own devices, say, on the

We can value Rousseau's insights and the role that intuition, experience, and feelings play in the development of the child, but they are not enough to insure the development of the good, morally developed child.

playground? Is it nurturing or defeating? Is it based on the active involvement of a caring parent or teacher or one who gives little attention to the child? Rousseau may have correctly gleaned that children have the seed of morality in them, but he failed to recognize the value of interactions with caring adults, teachers, and other students and the importance of good civil practices in developing the good child.

As an example, Daniel Goleman, in his book *Emotional Intelligence* (1995), reported that two-year-old children who have been raised in nurturing homes try to comfort a friend who is crying. Children who have been abused or neglected early in their life tend to yell at or hit crying children. Without a range of positive experiences from nurturing parents, the neglected children had

few compassionate or comforting skills to draw upon. The same notion applies in the development of civility within the school and community. If children do not see significant adults treating others with kindness and civility, they will be less likely to act in a civil manner toward others within the school environment. Children pick up on what is valued. If kindness and caring is modeled, discussed and valued, they are more likely to develop habits of kindness and caring. Children learn from what they see, what they are taught, and what they experience. Damon continues, "Simply put, children cannot learn wholly on their own; for intellectual growth [and we would argue growth in becoming civil people] they need to be instructed, prodded, challenged, corrected, and assisted by people who are trying to teach them something" (p. 105).

To maintain and develop a caring community for everyone, we need to insure that newer members of that community, our children, develop a commitment to it. We must instruct and lead not just the intellect of students, but their moral and social processes as well. We must insist on practices that lead to the formation of a good learning and caring community in which we will all feel safe and happy to live. Of course, children need time to explore ideas and play—that's a crucial tool in learning—but they also need to develop the habits of civility: being respectful, responsible, and caring, all of which is learned by adult modeling, teaching, and interaction with others. Consider the following example.

A School Community That Understands

Lebanon High School, a suburban school outside of Pittsburgh, was visited by one of the authors during a site evaluation for the National Schools of Character program. The students provided an excellent example of civility during a classroom discussion. In a junior-level English class, students were exchanging their views on a recently completed reading assignment. The class seemed to represent the diversity of the high school in ethnicity and represented a great variety of viewpoints. The observer heard statements such as, "I understand your point. However, I believe you could interpret that statement as saying..." "OK, I can accept your opinion, but I see the author supporting..." "I can agree with you about the main point and I would like to suggest that..."

As the discussion unfolded without more than a few words from the teacher, the observer was impressed to note the remarkably well-developed discussion skills displayed by the students that supported a civil dialogue. The students were demonstrating excellent attention to the ideas of classmates. There was a high level of synthesis and analysis taking place with the reading assignment and the ideas of peers. Students were demonstrating the skill of reframing the statements of others to show respect and understanding of their classmates' ideas. All of this was taking place while the participants held strong attachment to personal opinions. The discussion clarified a number of points of clear disagreement within the class. At the conclusion of the class, the observer was pleased to recognize that not a single insult or put-down had been exchanged in a discussion that included meaningful energy and vastly different points of view.

This class occurred just prior to lunch, and with the teacher's approval, the observer asked that any students who were willing to stay behind for a few minutes of extra discussion. About 18 of the 25 students stayed behind and reflected with the observer on his

We must instruct and lead not just the intellect of students, but their moral and social processes as well.

notes about the class. From this discussion, several themes became very clear. The students confirmed the class was a conventional track English class and did not have an honors or AP designation. The discussion format was considered the norm of the school and not just the result of one exceptional English teacher. The students acknowledged that their school experience had included lessons on classroom discussion standards since elementary school. Teachers across the district, some more than others, were noted to emphasize discussion skill lessons at the beginning of every school year. Most of the students recognized their own appreciation of the excellent civil standards that were established, taught and reinforced by the district teachers.

Lebanon High School provides a great example of how a school (the whole district) can purposefully identify skills that support civility, teach those skills that clearly include specific behaviors for civil classroom dialogue and reinforce the instruction of those skills over time and all academic disciplines. With this focus on civil classroom behavior, Lebanon High School students were demonstrating the habit of civil dialogue and were growing in their appreciation of the positive value and ethic of maintaining civil classrooms.

In conclusion, it is up to us as educators to activate the "moral circuitry" already present in children's systems and to teach them and encourage them to become the moral citizens they were born to be. Our children come to us with the necessary "wiring" to become moral, kind, caring, people. It is up to us to apply what we know about the emotional and intellectual needs of children to ensure that the climate we provide them in school will be sufficient to enable them to achieve academically and civilly.

CHAPTER 3

Developing
the Civil Climate

The core problem facing our schools is a moral one. All the other problems derive from it.... If they [students] don't learn habits of courage and justice, curriculums designed to improve their self-esteem won't stop the epidemic of extortion, bullying, and violence; neither will courses designed to make them more sensitive to diversity.... If they don't acquire intellectual virtues such as commitment to learning, objectivity, respect for the truth, and humility in the face of facts, then critical-thinking strategies will only amount to one more gimmick in the curriculum (p. 225).

—William Kilpatrick
Why Johnny Can't Tell Right From Wrong **(1992)**

William Kilpatrick points out clearly the moral problem facing our schools. He also notes that it has recuperative potential. Remedying this problem, he says, calls for the provision of a moral/civil environment in schools for all students. Such an environment requires, as we have noted, good modeling and teaching on the part of the adults to help children develop the basic habits of civility in addition to aiding them in their intellectual understanding of ideas and issues that promote civility. James Kauffman and Harold Burbach (1997) recognize the importance of these initial civilities:

At a minimum, the kind of social climate we envision is one in which everyone, teachers and students alike, treats others with consideration and respect and in which mannerly behavior and small courtesies are the norm. More optimistically, we believe that a classroom where civility holds sway is one that is well on its way to facilitating classroom cooperation, responsible self-governance, and democratic living (p. 322).

What We Do Matters

The establishment and modeling of basic norms of civility prompts a school to operate as a good community, thus enabling students to function well within the dynamics of the community. But it is not enough merely to prompt students. Educators, as noted in the previous chapter, must recognize the importance of modeling good habits and working with students so they can develop such behaviors themselves. If we insist that students be fair and honest, we must strive to be fair and honest. If we desire that students be caring, we must be caring. If we want students to be polite, we must be polite. Remember, civility will not simply be taught—it must also be caught.

Borrowing from the field of character education, we cite Marvin Berkowitz (2002), who has determined seven keys for effective character development based on research literature to date. We believe his work has much to offer us as we consider the development of the civil school. The seven practices are:

1. **How people treat the child.** Is the child treated benevolently and with respect? Is the environment psychologically supportive and promotive of pro-social relationships?
2. **How significant others treat other people in the child's presence.** Cleaning up our acts and walking the talk is necessary for character education to be effective.
3. **The school staff needs to expect good character of all its members.** Character needs to be a clear priority and expectation for all the stakeholders within a school.
4. **The school staff must espouse positive character.** We must practice what we preach, but also preach what we practice.
5. **We must provide opportunities for children to practice good character.** This will involve perspective taking, critical thinking and conflict resolution as well as peer mediation, student self-governance and charitable activities.
6. **Students need opportunities to reason about, debate and reflect on moral issues within the curriculum.** We must work to have students focus on issues of character and morality.
7. **Parents should be actively and positively involved in the school's character education efforts** (pp. 58-61).

Notice how the first four practices and the last one apply directly to the modeling and habits of civility. Berkowitz further noted that students need time to work together, to reflect and discuss ideas, and to serve others in the school and community. But as a prerequisite to all curriculum presentations, students need order and structure. This should not be seen as punitive in regard to a child's moral and social development, but rather as foundational in a child's moral and social development. Developing guidelines through the establishment of practices that promote the habits of civility helps ensure order and structure, and therefore a good community. Common sense tells us children who are expected to have habits of civility, which thereby nurture habits of respect, responsibility, perseverance, and similar traits, are more likely to be successful in school and in life than those who have not had instruction in civility. Perhaps the following illustrates this point. One of the authors has, on occasion, worked with business leaders within communities. He usually asks the group how many of them have dismissed an employee because the employee was intellectually unable to do the job he or she was hired to do. Rarely will anyone raise a hand. He then asks how many of them have dismissed an employee because the person lacked habits of civility such as being courteous or respectful toward others. Usually every hand is raised. The so-called "soft skills," or basic civilities, are now the "hard skills" that will determine the success of an employee and potentially a business. How can students hope to find and keep good career jobs if they don't have the basic civilities needed to succeed socially and intellectually within a work environment?

The so-called "soft skills," or basic civilities, are now the "hard skills" that will determine the success of an employee and potentially a business.

We Must Lead

However, we as the adults are in charge of raising and educating the next generation. We must also acknowledge that in general over the last 25 years, we have become more lax in our expectations of basic civility within the general culture, which also includes the school. The lack of consistency, proper instruction, and modeling for our youth has created a climate where standards have not been taught and reinforced as effectively as they might have been. We are slacking in our teaching and modeling of the "micro" aspects of civility such as courtesy and respect. This in turn will impact on our "macro" understanding of the moral and civil issues we will face. All children are born with certain dispositions that can be developed, with guidance, into civil behavior. However, if they are left without a guide—without a parent, teacher, or other role model who cares enough to act as a moral compass—they may drift toward a more negative and potentially destructive path.

To establish a safe and civil environment, we must first determine the steps and practices that will guide us in the formation of civility in our schools.

Children, for the most part, act based on what is expected of them. And if civil behavior is not expected of them, less than ideal behaviors may follow. This may, in turn, develop negative habits in children.

Based upon the efforts of children's parents, other adults and their early grade teachers, the majority of our students have been taught and have developed habits of being civil toward others. However, simply striving for a majority is not adequate. Just a few students and/or adults can have a negative impact on the majority to people in a community. All of our students deserve the opportunity to develop good habits of civility to assist them throughout their lives. Even if children are failing to receive and see civility modeled within the home and community, they can and do learn to separate the expectations from the home and the expectations of the school. When they walk through the doors of a school, civility must be modeled, taught and expected.

Our task is to help each child develop the habits that will promote civility in and, we hope, outside the school. In this manner, we help the child develop the habits that will promote acceptance and friendship among peers and adults. As the school climate of caring and civility grows, a safe and orderly environment should evolve, and the opportunity for academic and intellectual growth should occur. If a school lacks a civil climate, both intellectual and civil development will face difficulty. Intellectual and civil growth go hand in hand. One cannot exist without the other, for desired learning does not generally occur in chaos. Lack of civility hinders productivity in the school environment, as well as in the home. We as educators must make school civility a priority for all children, for they will struggle academically unless they are able to study and work within a civil, caring climate.

Think of your own experiences. As adults, we generally prefer schedules and structure, especially within our work environment. We enjoy a civil/caring workplace. We like to have friends at work who are kind and caring. It helps us do our work better when we generally know what to expect throughout the day and generally know how those around us will act. We also appreciate such a culture in the home. Why should we desire anything less for our children/students in school? To establish a safe and civil environment, we must first determine the steps and practices that will guide us in the formation of civility in our schools.

In nurturing self-disciplined, civil children, we need to establish boundaries and solid structures that promote virtuous behaviors. Emile Durkheim, the esteemed 19th-century sociologist, reminds us that "...solely by imposing limits can a child be liberated." This line of reasoning is more recently advanced by Christina Hoff Sommers in her book, *The War Against Boys* (2000). Sommers notes:

> **Far from being oppressive,** controlling, or constricting, the manners, instincts, and virtues we recognize in decent, considerate human beings—in the case of males, the manners, instincts, and virtues we associate with being a "gentleman"—are liberating. To educate, humanize and civilize a boy is to allow him to make the most of himself (p. 197).

Similarly, by imposing limits of what is acceptable and unacceptable in schools through the generation of civil practices, students will cultivate the habits needed as prerequisites for becoming good students and citizens. Let us examine a single civil practice, the development of punctuality.

As a society, we value punctuality because its practice demonstrates a willingness to consider the needs of others. It is a key factor in making a good impression in a job interview and in keeping a job. The issue of punctuality shows why having a tardy rule and insisting that students and teachers strive for timely attendance to school and class is so important. Yet the reasons, at least initially, why students (and some teachers) will choose not to be tardy will vary. Many will comply because tardiness has been considered rude to others and inappropriate in their homes. They have already developed the habit of punctuality and expect it of themselves. Others may comply because they recognize if students are habitually late, no serious instruction can occur. A small number will comply because of the potential consequences that result from being tardy to class. An athlete knows that the coach will suspend him or her from a game for being consistently tardy to class or practice. Athletes do not want to face the consequence of being late, though without that consequence, the young athletes may not put great attention on being punctual. Although some people may follow the rules to avoid consequences, this is not where we want students or adults to remain. It may be an acceptable first step toward developing a habit of punctuality, but this is not the final motivation for punctuality that we envision. Our goal is to have them recognize the value and importance of punctuality to themselves and others, as well as other practices that promote civility. Therefore we as educators must, through our efforts and having students practice and reflect, help them develop the habit of punctuality and the related sense of responsibility and commitment to themselves and the school community.

Aristotle Helps Us Again

Aristotle suggests this in the *Nicomachean Ethics,* in which he describes two kinds of virtue. He describes intellectual virtue as the contemplative side of virtue, which is experienced through thinking and reflecting on ideas. Take punctuality again. A teacher could ask students to reflect on why punctuality at school is important. He could provide an activity in which students discuss how they have felt when others have been tardy in fulfilling an obligation. Perhaps a writing assignment could be assigned on the importance of developing the habit of punctuality. Learning to think clearly and applying logic to social and moral concerns help enhance intellectual virtue and, hopefully, an intellectual understanding on the importance of civility. But before intellectual virtue can develop, one needs to begin the process of habit development. One needs, as noted earlier, "the that," which Aristotle calls moral virtue.

To review, Aristotle's concept of moral virtue is established and sustained through the formulation and practice of good habits and the obvious reflection that goes along with the practice and development of good habits. For example, a child might recognize that people who practice basic civilities tend to treat each other with greater kindness. That will benefit the child as he becomes older and takes his place in society. Successful educators and adults model and demand punctuality. They work hard to develop in students the habit of punctuality. Schools develop tardy rules and enforce them as needed with the hope that, via practice, students will develop the habits of punctuality. Developing habits of civility would include, but are not limited to, being punctual, respectful, responsible, and caring. To extend this ideal to school, we need to formulate a vision of civility and then determine the practices needed to develop or reinforce the habits of civility. Consider the following:

> **Goal**—To develop a habit of punctuality by being on time to class and other school obligations.
>
> **Expectation**—Students will exhibit punctuality throughout the school day.
>
> **Practices**—Arrive at school on time. Observe the tardy rule to class. Enter the class and be seated before the tardy bell rings.

Through the practices and the development of good habits, students and adults are able to forge a civil climate. Both educators and students deserve to work in a nurturing climate where the students and adults are caring, respectful, and civil toward each other. A school's climate determines the success we will have in germinating in some students and reinforcing in others the respect, self-discipline, and other practices which lead to a civil climate. Let us now consider how teachers and students can begin to enhance a school's climate.

The Importance of Climate

James Leming presents the connection between school climate, rules and civil practices in an article entitled "In Search of Effective Character Education" (1993). He writes:

> **Character develops within a social web or environment.** The nature of that environment, the messages it sends to individuals, and the behaviors it encourages and discourages, are important factors to consider in character education. Clear rules of conduct, student ownership of those rules, a supportive environment and satisfaction resulting from complying with the norms of the environment shape behavior (p. 69).

The climate of a school is a clear reflection of its inhabitants. Generally, a school with a civil climate has educators and students who comply with the norms of the school and therefore enjoy being at school. Schools with civility have people who want to build relationships with each other. Jim Sweeney notes in *Tips for Improving School Climate* (1988):

Climate is a term used to describe how people feel about their school. It is a combination of beliefs, values, and attitudes shared by students, teachers, administrators, parents, bus drivers, office personnel, custodians, cafeteria workers, and others who play an important role in the life of the school. When a school has a "winning climate," people feel proud, connected, and committed. They support, help, and care for each other. When the climate is right, there is a certain joy in coming to school, either to teach or to learn (p.1).

Larry Nucci (2001), one of the foremost researchers in moral development, has formulated some guidelines for schools to consider when developing a comprehensive vision of a good school climate. He reminds us that a climate of acceptance and warmth is essential at any grade level but especially so at the preschool through primary years. "Because children are in the early phase of integrating affect within their moral and personal schemas, it is important that positive affect be overly manifest within the school context" (p. 148). Children at this age are open to displays of warmth and also negatively impacted by anger from adults. Nucci continues arguing that we, "would want to do whatever possible to enable young children to construct a view of the world as benevolent and fair so that they might construct an orientation of 'goodwill' towards others" (p. 148). In middle childhood and early adolescence (grades 3-8) Nucci states, "The climate of acceptance and warmth that characterized the good preschool is also essential at the elementary and middle school levels. Children at this age range are less dependent on adults but they still look to them for education and social stability" (p. 149). Teachers must work hard to see that all students, regardless of academic abilities or social skills (being shy, nerdy, preppie, etc.), are included within the life of the school. Nucci reminds us that, "Being made to look dumb in class or being made the outsider on the playground is not simply a problem of peer culture but of the school and its values" (p. 150).

Within adolescence (high school) Nucci recommends, "The social climate of the high school should continue to underscore the basic elements of safety and academic and social participation discussed in regard to earlier grade levels. Integrated participation of students is particularly important at the high school level in order to offset the tendencies toward segregation into cliques and crowds that characterize peer relations at this age" (p. 150). He recommends promoting a climate in which people from diverse interests and abilities are interacting with each other. Since many of our contemporary high schools are so large, "houses" or communities can be established within school to help build relationships. "In general, these strategies use a common set of courses (e.g., English, history) or a class period (e.g., homeroom) as a way of identifying 'houses' or communities within the school. Teachers and students within a given house remain together for at least one academic year and may use specified times throughout the year to address or discuss social issues collectively" (p. 151). One of the authors has visited a high school that tried to keep the "house" together throughout the entire high school experience. As a point

of reference, it is not just high schools that have recognized the importance of building community within the academic experience. Yale University uses its student dorms as "colleges." Freshmen remain in their college cohort for all kinds of community-building and service activities during their college years. Even if a student moves off campus, they are still "assigned" to this college and are encouraged to participate in various activities of the group. All of this is done to advance a sense of community within the college.

Although there are differences in approaches we might take to formulating a civil climate, we should recognize that when a school has a civil climate, people interact warmly and positively, care about each other, and try to formulate a strong sense of community. This is what all educators and students deserve. To achieve this climate, a school must have practices that are followed and supported by both teachers and students. A focus on modeling and teaching civility results in a good, fertile climate for intellectual and social growth.

Educators play a most fundamental part in this process by modeling appropriate social behavior, as previously discussed. Through their modeling and expectations, they plant seeds that they hope will bear the fruit of good behavior. For some students, the modeling of good behavior, the opportunity to practice and develop habits of civility (e.g., punctuality) are enough to engender persistent good habits. Other students want to see what will happen when they don't follow certain rules and must be shown the consequences of their actions. No matter—a good school helps young people grow into good citizens through instruction, modeling, and an insistence on civility for the betterment of everyone in the school.

One way to foster the development of a good climate is to understand the meaning and differences between rules and practices. *The New World Dictionary of the American Language* (1986) defines *rule* as: "an authoritative regulation for action, conduct, method, procedure, arrangement, etc. [the rules of the school]." *Practice* is defined as: "to do or engage in frequently or usually; make a habit or custom of, to do repeatedly in order to learn or become proficient; exercise or drill oneself."

Rules regulate and establish rights and wrongs. For example, we may establish the rule "No fighting in our school," or "No cursing at others in our school." These rules are designed to establish the boundaries of acceptable behavior. We may also consider these rules the safety limits of what is acceptable. The rules are not designed to promote civility, but only to limit practices that destroy or impede practices that promote civility. Individuals who choose to violate these rules will face consequences for their acts (Chapter 5). Practices are the habits that we wish to model and develop in students to meet the expectation of establishing a civil school. Now, this is very important. The establishment of rules will not help us establish the civil school. They will only inform us of the boundaries of acceptable behavior in the school or classroom. We have to go beyond this to establish the civil climate. The establishment of practices based upon expectations of civility leads the development of habits of civility. For example, the expectation to "be respectful" is incomplete in providing direction unless practices—using polite language such as *please, thank you, excuse me* or *pardon me* and holding the door for those walking behind you—are taught and modeled and habituated. The failure to cultivate good habits such as respect and responsibility dooms a child to actions based on impulses, without the attributes needed to develop into a good citizen.

Developing Consistent Practices

The establishment of expectations and the subsequent practices are beneficial to the establishment of the civil school. Following consistent civil practices is the primary means to achieve self-control in students, which allows all students a civil, orderly environment in which to pursue their education.

To learn more about this, we turn to Dr. Harry and Tripi Wong's work, *The First Days of School* (1991). They write:

1. The most successful classes are those where the teacher has a clear idea of what is expected from the students and the students know what the teacher expects from them.
2. Expectations can be stated as rules.
3. Rules are expectations of appropriate student behavior.
4. After thorough deliberation, decide on your rules and write them down or post them before the first days of school.
5. Communicate clearly to your students what you expect as appropriate behavior.
6. It is easier to maintain good behavior than to change inappropriate behavior that has become established.
7. Rules immediately create a work-oriented atmosphere (p. 143).

Note the importance that the word "expectations" plays in the Wongs' use of rules. We are going to differ from the Wongs but recognize the importance of their insights. Rules and expectations are both needed for a school. Our focus will be on *the establishment of expectations that will guide us in forging our practices to promote the civil climate*. The establishment of expectations will determine the practices and the subsequent posting of the expectations and practices to focus our behavior on standards of excellence. For example, the expectation "We respect ourselves and others within the school" provides for us the standard that we all should strive to obtain. To develop consistent practices in the civil school, we recommend using the following outline. The outline will examine how we can develop the habits that lead to respectful behavior in the school.

- First we must determine the expectation of appropriate behavior in our school. Borrowing from the above, we establish our expectation: **We respect ourselves and others within the school.**

- We must next determine the practices that will help the students and adults reach the standards established in the expectations. Following are several practices which, if followed, would promote respect for ourselves and others within the school:
  We listen while others are talking.
  We use polite language such as please, thank you, may I, excuse me.
  We raise our hands to speak and put them down when someone is recognized.
  We do not verbally or physically harm others.

- We highlight the expectation: **We respect ourselves and others within the school.** We also post the practices beneath the expectation and post them throughout the school.

We respect ourselves and others within the school.

- **We use polite language such as *please, thank you, may I, excuse me.***
- In large groups, we raise our hands to speak and put them down when someone is recognized. In small groups we try not to interrupt others.
- We do not verbally or physically harm others.

This outline offers several advantages for the teacher or staff who wish to develop a more civil climate. First, it requires us to consider the expectations for our students and ourselves. Secondly, it requires us to determine practices that we, as well as our students, should do to develop the habit of being respectful. (Note: We are placing much of this responsibility on the teacher, but students are capable of providing and in some cases determining the practices need within the classroom and school to promote civility. We will talk more about this later.) In most cases, we would urge that three or four practices be listed under the statement of the expectation. Let us now examine how two teachers utilized expectations and practices to develop the civil climate in their classes.

CHAPTER 4

Practices Breathe Life into Civility

As we said in the last chapter, rules (standards) are different from expectation and practices (behaviors). Every school has rules that communicate the boundaries of acceptable behavior, (e.g., no fighting and walk, do not run, in the halls). These rules are hopefully formulated to limit behavior that may pose a danger (emotionally or physically) to a child in a school. Expectations and their subsequent practices help establish the behaviors and habits that a civil school must have. Only with the establishment of a civil climate will the intellectual and social flourishing of those in the school community occur. Unfortunately, not every expectation about respect and civility comes with a list of practices that make clear what specific behavior is expected, and *it is the practice of civil behavior that will lead to habits of civility.* Young people always respond better when they're asked to do a specific thing, rather than meet a vague objective. If you say, "I want this room cleaned up," will it end up as you would like it to be? Or do you have better success when you say, "I want the coats hung up, the books on the shelf, the chairs straightened, and all the trash in the wastebasket"? We already know the answer to that. If children know *specifically* what they're supposed to do, and know how to do it, most of them will, at least eventually, comply and contribute.

The Importance of Habits

A civil environment that focuses on caring and consistency is essential for a child to develop a sense of security and order in his or her life. James Q. Wilson, in his work, *The Moral Sense* (1993), takes a strong position:

> **...habits, routine ways of acting,** each rather unimportant in itself, but taken together, producing action on behalf of quite important sensibilities. For example: the habit of courtesy (which over the long run alerts us to the feelings of others), the habit of punctuality (which disposes us to be dutiful in the exercise of our responsibilities and confirms to others that we have a sense of duty), and the habit of practice (by which we master skills and proclaim to others that we are capable of excellence) (p. 241).

The little habits, practiced daily, help a school function smoothly and mold the civility and character of youth and adults, which makes a great deal of difference in the life of the child. Consistent rules and practices "set the table" for all future civility-developing efforts.

Unfortunately, some educators argue that establishing good practices and following rules and civil practices aren't all that important. For example, Steve Farkas and Jean Johnson from the research firm Public Agenda conducted a survey entitled *Different Drummers: How Teachers of Teachers View Public Education* (1997). The study involved surveying professors of education who were responsible for training teachers for our schools. The study addressed various topics, one of which was what "professors of education think 'absolutely essential' qualities of a teacher are." In other words, what essential qualities or classroom practices should a teacher have in order to be successful. Some of their conclusions are listed below.

37% To maintain classroom order and discipline
19% To stress correct spelling, punctuation and grammar
12% To expect students to be neat, on time and polite

We beg to disagree with the professors. We feel that maintaining classroom order and discipline, expecting students to be neat, on time and polite, as well as the development of basic skills of written communication, are *essential* classroom practices and expectations. How can children learn unless there is structure and expectations of basic intellectual and social civility within a class?

Here's a tough question: When do students generally get into trouble—during times of direct instruction or during transitions? Like most educators, you probably answered the latter. If talking and impolite behavior routinely get out of hand during transitions, the problem is a procedural one, which can be remedied with clear-cut practices designed to promote civility. Students are not thinking "I have to remember to respect others" when they pass up their test papers and leave the classroom. A teacher who wants to promote civility will not only be modeling and saying, "Respect others, students," she will be reminding her students of, for example, the class practices for handing up papers: "We are out of class time. Please pass your papers to the person in front of you and then get your materials together to prepare for dismissal. Thanks for a great day." In this classroom, clearly defined practices let students know how they're supposed to behave; the teacher's brief reminder keeps everyone on track.

> *We must model what we expect of our children. If we want children to be respectful, then we must be respectful.*

The Common Expectation: Respect Others

Let's examine a common expectation within school: "Respect others." That, or perhaps "Treat everyone with respect," is expected and in some cases, posted as an expectation in thousands of schools across the country. Its objective is to yield a body of students (and hopefully, teachers) who speak courteously to everyone, are on time and prepared for class, and don't intrude in others' space or impose on others' privacy. But most students, especially young ones, don't read all that into this expectation. In all grade levels, some students come from homes where family members don't show respect for one another, and the whole concept is new. So how can we lead students into "treating everyone with respect"? First, we must model what we expect of our children. If we want children to be respectful, then we must be respectful. If we want them to be responsible, we must seek to be responsible. At the same time we are modeling the expectations, we can tell and remind students that we expect respectful *behavior*. Then we explain and demonstrate what respectful behavior looks, sounds, and feels like.

Perhaps we seek their input, insights, and modeling of what being respectful looks and sounds like. Afterwards we might post the expectation "Treat others with respect" and give practices underneath the rule that, if followed, will develop and reinforce the habit(s) of being respectful. Some educators choose to have their students assist them in the development of classroom standards and civil practices. This, too, can be very effective and will be discussed later in this chapter.

An excellent methodology to help teachers organize the development of civil practices is provided by C. Evertson (et. al) in *Organizing and Managing the Elementary School Classroom* (1981), published by the Research and Development Center for Teacher Education at the University of Texas at Austin. This work recognizes that actions designed to develop habits in students are important to help them learn to follow basic expectations that, if followed, would promote civility. Observe how this project establishes an expectation and then offers guidelines to help the expectation become internalized by the teacher as well as the child.

1. **Be polite and helpful.** This may be worded in various ways (e.g., be considerate of others; be courteous). Children must be given examples for this rule to have meaning. They must learn [what to do] to be polite and helpful in dealing with adults and each other.

2. **Take care of our school.** This is another very general rule that the teacher must think through before using. The teacher may want to include positive examples, such as picking up trash in the halls or on the school grounds, returning library books on time, and/or such rigidly stated things as not marking on walls, desks, or school books. The teacher must be sure to discuss and follow up with the class whatever detailed behavior is expected from this rule as well as consequences for *not* following the rule (p. 41).

Both our approach and the Texas Project reveal that just stating the expectation isn't enough to develop civility in students. Teachers working individually, with their students, or as a school must determine the practices needed to help students understand and develop good habits that promote civility as a natural part of their day. Determine the expectations, and then develop and provide some practices that give meaning to this expectation.

So far, the discussion has chiefly addressed expectation and practices in the domain of educators. Can students help to determine expectations and civil practices? Absolutely! Students as young as three to five years of age know about the importance of civil practices. Robert Marzano, in his work *Classroom Management That Works: Research-Based Strategies for Every Teacher* (2003), conducted a meta-analysis (a technique for quantitatively synthesizing the findings from a number of studies) on the importance of establishing rules and procedures (we prefer the term practices, but for all practical purposes, the terms are interchangeable) for assisting in classroom management. He concluded:

> **Research and theory,** then, support the intuitive notion that well-articulated rules and procedures that are negotiated with students are a critical aspect of classroom management affecting not only the behavior of students but also their academic achievement (p. 17).

The following approaches utilize students' input in developing a civil classroom:

An Elementary Approach

Retired elementary educator Cynthia Vincent had a very simple belief. If all adults and children in the class were civil and caring to each other, the school year would be more enjoyable and the class would meet its academic goals. Building on this philosophy, she modeled and implemented civil practices based on her rules about being respectful, responsible, and caring toward themselves and others as the key components of civility. She started out the school year on the first day by having the words *Respect, Responsibility,* and *Caring* posted on her three bulletin boards. She then asked each student what he or she did at home and at school to practice being respectful, responsible, and caring. Each idea was discussed in depth. Afterward, the students created art that illustrated them practicing respect, responsibility, and caring. This art was then used to complete the bulletin boards. Ms. Vincent compiled her and her students' ideas into a list of civil practices they all would follow in the classroom and other school areas. Generally she provided three or four practices under each expectation (e.g., "Be respectful.").

On the second day of school, these students began their practices of being respectful, responsible, and caring. They role-played incidents when saying "thank you" or "excuse me" would be the appropriate response. They practiced walking quietly down the hall to show respect for other classes. The practices to develop habits of civility were continued diligently through the week. During this time, she read stories or narratives to the students on the importance of civility (e.g., some of George Washington's rules on civil behavior). Her key focus was on developing the habits and having students reflect on these habits. After the first week, the students had begun to internalize many of the habits of civility that would allow them to be successful in school. An environment that was good for students as well as the teacher deliberately evolved. Ms. Vincent continued the focus by having a meeting at the beginning of each school day in order for students to talk about issues and concerns as well as what they could do to be respectful and responsible that day. Time was taken to thank others for what they had done the previous day. Through her modeling and practices, the message was sent that civility was not part of the "hidden curriculum" but was the catalyst to drive the curriculum.

Any "backsliding" regarding civility was discussed over a class meeting at the beginning of the day or if a more serious incident occurred, immediately. The students were asked to reflect upon what had been occurring in the classroom and offer suggestions on how to solve the present problem. Ideas were taken, entertained and discussed. The classroom practices were reviewed for further reinforcement. Even at elementary ages, children are capable of evaluating their behavior and contributing to the class objectives; they fully participated in these class meetings. Practices promoting civility that were not being followed consistently were highlighted and extra effort was required. In general, this was not an everyday occurrence, but if the situation required a class meeting to refocus on our need for civility, then time was taken out of the regular instructional time.

Some might say that taking so much time at the beginning of the year, at the beginning of each day and, if needed, during the normal school day, would be wasting valuable instructional time. Ms. Vincent felt that only by addressing issues of civility combined

After the first week, the students had begun to internalize many of the habits of civility that would allow them to be successful in school.

with having a classroom that promoted a caring attitude toward others could she meet her academic goals. By modeling and implementing practices for proper behavior in class, Ms. Vincent had a respectful and caring environment in which to teach, and the students "lived" in an environment that emphasized social and intellectual learning. Finally, as students continued growing in their civil behavior, they were recognized for their success. Letters were sent home to the parents, and the entire class occasionally celebrated wonderful acts of civility and kindness around the school or within the community. However, most of the time a quiet word, a pat on a shoulder, a smile, or a nod between the teacher and the child was more than enough recognition.

The Class Meeting

The "class meeting" can be an essential part of a civil school. Children often have issues that we, as adults, may not see. A class meeting is a wonderful time to address some of these issues. Ruth Sidney Charney's work is the best we have seen on this topic. In her book, *Teaching Children to Care: Management in the Responsive Classroom* (1992), Charney outlines the importance and some strategies in promoting a weekly class or morning meeting. Some of her class meeting practices and guidelines are:

- Meeting once a week at a regular time gives children time to digest and reflect, and makes the procedure special.
- Keep time during the meeting. The meeting should last only a pre-determined amount of time.
- Meet in a circle so everyone can see each other.
- Set up a weekly agenda.
- The teacher sets the tone, begins and ends the meeting, and keeps the group focused on the topic and the meeting rules. (pp. 78-79)

Charney has also established steps for problem-solving in the meetings. These steps are as follows:

- Introduce the problem and review the rules.
- Gather information.
- Begin discussion: "What do you need in order to...?"
- Propose solutions.
- Choose a solution.
- Choose a consequence.
- Close the meeting. (p. 80)

Civility modeled by the teacher and expected of the students is the standard of behavior on which any good meeting must be based. We strongly recommend that anyone who is serious about becoming competent in holding daily, regular or "needed" classroom meetings should read Charney's work.

A Secondary Approach

Charlie Abourjilie was hired in January 2002 to become the first Director of Character Education for the state of North Carolina. Abourjilie was selected due to his excellence as a classroom teacher and because of his wonderful book, *Developing Character for Classroom Success* (2001), which focused on helping teachers create a good classroom environment in the middle/high school. Abourjilie describes what he did to promote civility in his high school class, though this approach will work very well in the middle grades and can be adjusted "down" for any grade. Here are some of his key ideas from his book as well as his talks:

As a high school teacher, I think that the "civility" in my classroom starts with me, carries over to my students, then our class as a whole, and hopefully does not end. There are many approaches that secondary teachers take toward achieving a civil classroom. My approach begins with some of my philosophical beliefs—my attitude and vision for my classes:

For starters, *I am a role model* for my students—my children. What I do in front of my students is as important, if not more so, as what I say to them. (How I say things is also of great significance.)

Second, I realize that *I cannot control my children. I can truly only control myself* (and there are times for all of us when that isn't always easy). I can set the tone for my class. I, working with my students, establish the rules and civil practices for the class. I try to model respect and caring for each of the students in my classroom, and I expect the same from them in their actions toward me and their peers.

Third, and maybe most important, is my belief *that educating and contributing to the civil and moral development of children is based in large part on the quality of the relationships built and nurtured in my classroom.* The foundation for my relationship with my students is that I think of them, treat them, and teach them as if they are my own children—and my children need modeling, instruction and an opportunity to practice and develop habits of civility.

I don't think I ever use the word "civility" with my kids in class to describe or talk about our class atmosphere, but civility is what we are all about. We talk about building a sense of "community." We talk about and set the goals and ideals of our class being like a community—one based on respect, responsibility, honesty, caring, and the courage to do what is right, even if it is not popular. My students know that my classroom is "our classroom" and any success in there is based on what we do together—for ourselves and each other. Once the kids feel this sense of belonging and ownership, we have laid a solid foundation to build upon. Following are a few specific practices that should prove helpful in promoting civility in a classroom.

DISCIPLINE THAT IS FIRM, FAIR, RESPECTFUL AND RESPONSIBLE

Essential to developing solid relationships is structure, consistency, and expecting the best from every party involved in that relationship. To help ensure this, I establish the classroom civil practices that I want my students to perform daily, and then we practice those to make sure they are carried out correctly. For example, on the very first day of school, and on the next two or three, I have my kids practice coming into the classroom, sometimes three, four, or five times at the start of the period. I tell and show them how I want them to come in the classroom and what they are to do in those first minutes in the class, and then they do it repeatedly, until I think they get the point. Not every student likes this. Some may wonder what in the world is going on, but that is okay. My job is not to be popular—it is to establish the best possible learning environment for my children and then teach them to the best of my ability. Establishing civil practices and doing them until they become habits provide the stability and consistency that all children want and need. Getting it right at the beginning helps me immeasurably throughout the course of the year.

HANDSHAKE

For me, it starts at the door of the classroom, from the very first day, even before the bell rings to start class. Every day, before each class, I stand outside my doorway waiting to greet my students with a smile and a handshake. Many handshakes soon turn to high-fives, pats on the back, and often hugs. Many years ago I remember hearing Dr. Harry Wong talk about standing in the doorway and shaking students' hands. I gave it a try and since that time have seen the magic grow. By greeting my children with a handshake and smile every day, gives me a chance to give each child some individual, personal attention. It is often a silent communication that says "how are you?" and "I'm here for you." No child goes unnoticed. I get to gauge where each child is on that day in terms of mood, attitude, and physical well-being. I get the chance to perhaps brighten their day with a sincere "Hello, how are you?" and more often than not my kids brighten and energize *my* day. My kids come to expect and want that greeting. I've had kids who would not enter the room until they got their handshake.

THANK YOU

Is there any more important, more positive two-word phrase in our language? We probably all teach our own children at home to say "thank you" to everyone any time we receive something, just as you were probably reminded hundreds of times as a child: "What do you say?" Most of us probably try to model at home for our children, but how often do we model it at school by saying "thank you" to our students and have them work to develop the habit of saying to others within the school community? Once again, something so simple can make all the difference in the world in your classroom climate and in relationships with your students!

CONCLUSION

Classroom civility does not come from me being a dictator and ruling with an iron fist. As the teacher and leader in the classroom, I have the choice to teach and create the atmosphere by inducing fear or by building relationships. Real civility and community is fostered by building relationships and expecting the best from my children and myself. It doesn't happen overnight, but it begins in those first few moments of personal interaction with your kids. We must teach our children and participate with our children in working together, showing respect for self and others, accepting responsibility and showing empathy. The goal must be more than to simply have our kids behave while they are in class. Civility, a sense belonging and feeling of being a part of something special, must come from within.

Both Cynthia Vincent and Charlie Abourjilie have established expectations for promoting a civil classroom at the outset of the school year. Both work with their students to help them understand the expectations and, more important, practices designed to promote and develop the civil classroom. Both of these educators are pro-active in their belief that it is better to establish and foster the habits of civility than to tolerate or encourage practices that may eventually lead to incivility in the classroom and, ultimately, serious consequences for the student(s). Unfortunately, not every student wants to join the program and we do need consequences for inappropriate actions in our schools. In the next chapter, we address this important tool in promoting civility.

CHAPTER 5

The Use of Consequences in Maintaining Civility

with Dr. David Wangaard

We live in a society that has consequences for certain behaviors deemed inappropriate. If you drive too fast, you will get a speeding ticket. If you are caught driving while drunk, you will probably lose your driver's license. If you fail to pay your taxes, you'll likely be caught and will have to pay the back taxes, plus a penalty. All of these actions have consequences. In order to function smoothly, a community must have rules/laws, as well as consequences for those who choose to break them. In this way the community, which seeks to promote cooperative, positive behavior, can impose negative consequences on those who continually choose not to follow the rules or expectations. Consequences should be a bit painful to be a strong reminder of possible outcomes for our negative actions. School rules are just as important as community rules, and efforts should be made to lead children into following school rules. Those who choose not to follow them need to face consequences.

In the many school districts around the country we have been involved with, we have found that most school personnel desire to help children develop good habits. They want to model and expect consistent practices to help students develop and maintain habits of civility. Most school personnel understand well that the development of a civil climate leads to less dependence on consequences as a means to order and discipline a class. Children who see civility modeled, taught, and practiced begin to apply or develop the habits of civility. We find examples of this in schools throughout the nation. For example, one elementary school in Charlotte, North Carolina, over several years reduced its office referrals from over 300 a year to 81 for the 2002-2003 school year. They have worked hard to model and develop a climate of caring and civility, but school leaders recognize that consequences for inappropriate actions are still needed for some of their students.

The Need for Accountability

Most educators recognize the need for accountability and, if necessary, consequences for students who continually choose to disrupt the learning environment. In this chapter, we offer guidelines on how to develop and apply consequences to those who choose to violate the civility within the school. This chapter will not satisfy everyone. Some (e.g., Rousseau) advocates may argue that if we let kids find their own way with minimal adult supervision, they will learn through trial and error and grow into solid students and citizens. We do need trial and error to help us learn right from wrong, and there are times when a child may need less adult supervision. However, this does not divorce adults from the life of the child. A child needs to learn and internalize morally sound actions and attitudes from adults who are committed to helping a child become a civil person.

Appropriate behavior should be expected and exemplified by the child, even when he or she is away from immediate supervision. An acquaintance told one of the authors that when her teenagers left the house, she inquired where they were going, whom they would be with, and when they would be home. The teens also left with one rule: "Have responsible fun—no drinking, drugs, or sex!" The teens laughed about this, but their parents' insistence that habits of respect and responsibility to others and themselves—which was the point of their rule—were reinforced by this reminder. Children need the constant involvement of parents and other adults to keep them acting with good judgment, even when pressured by peers. Children need a moral compass.

Modeling right conduct and developing good habits are critical practices in developing civil children, and it takes a lot of

Most educators recognize the need for accountability and, if necessary, consequences for students who continually choose to disrupt the learning environment.

practice. As a parent, how many times have you reminded your children to say "please"? Modeling for and discussions about expectations help develop habits of civility in our children. However, sometimes this is not enough. Some children choose to act inappropriately. Sometimes it is a minor infraction. Other times it is more severe and can be physically and emotionally hurtful to others. It is times like this when the consequences of one's inappropriate actions must be confronted. Learning that there are consequences for certain negative behaviors has a vital place in building the social and moral character of our youth. James Q. Wilson, in *The Moral Sense* (1993), notes:

> **Testing limits is a way of asserting selfhood.** Maintaining limits is a way of asserting community. If the limits are asserted weakly, uncertainly, or apologetically, their effects must surely be weaker than if they are asserted boldly, confidently and persuasively (p. 9).

In *What Works in Schools: Translating Research Into Action* (2003), Robert Marzano examined factors that contribute to a successful school. One of his chapters addressed the use of disciplinary techniques in classroom behavior. Citing a meta-analysis done by Scott Stage and David Quiroz (1997) Marzano noted that the researchers divided disciplinary techniques into four categories. He defined these categories as: 1) reinforcement, 2) punishment, 3) no immediate consequences, and 4) combined punishment and reinforcement.

> **Disciplinary techniques that fall into the category *reinforcement*** involve some type of recognition or reward for positive behavior or timely cessation of negative behavior. Practices classified as *punishment* involve some type of negative consequences (e.g., loss of privileges, time-out) for inappropriate behavior. Interventions classified as *no immediate consequence* do not involve immediate consequences for inappropriate behavior but do involve some type of reminder when an inappropriate behavior appears imminent. For example, the teacher might remind a student who typically acts out at recess that she should remember to keep herself under control. Finally, the category of *combined punishment and reinforcement* involves recognition or reward in conjunction with consequences for inappropriate behavior (p. 90).

The following figure (p. 91) represents the summary of the data:

Disciplinary Technique	% Decrease in Disruptive Behavior
Reinforcement	31
Punishment	25
No immediate consequence	24
Punishment and reinforcement	33

The use of reinforcement, and punishment and reinforcement have the greatest impact in reducing disruptive behaviors. Therefore, the use of reinforcement that recognizes and rewards positive (civil) behavior combined with consequences for behavior that violates the civil norms of the classroom are important tools in facilitating the development of a civil classroom. We must work hard to develop the habits that promote civility but we must also not refrain from the use of consequences for actions that violate our civil norms.

Considering Consequences

Let's briefly examine the definition of consequence. According to *The New World Dictionary of the American Language, Second College Edition* (1986), *consequence* is defined as: "1. a result of an action, process, etc., outcome, effect. 2. a logical result or conclusion: inference." For example, if one assumes the consequences of one's actions, one will accept the "results of one's actions." Awareness of consequences implies that, if one chooses to misbehave, one will accept the logical result (punishment) for one's actions. If I choose to break the rule and not pay my federal taxes, I may face a consequence of a court hearing with subsequent penalties based on my rule breaking.

Consider the possibility of this statement of practice in a middle or high school. "Students who continue to disrupt the learning environment by breaking rules that foster the physical and social safety of others will face consequences." The disruption(s) may include cursing at students or teachers, threatening others, hitting others, and other acts inappropriate to a civil environment. Many schools have such a statement in their student handbook. The question is whether we have and enforce consequences that are quickly implemented when rules are violated.

We recognize that attending school is a right for all children regardless of their physical and/or emotional difficulties. However, attending a civil school is a privilege that all adults and children deserve. This privilege assumes that the adults and students do their duty in promoting a civil climate. If disruptive behavior or serious rule violation is tolerated or ignored, then what are the potential civil and academic outcomes for the school? Furthermore, what is the message that is being sent to those who continually violate the standards of civility within the school? We should also recognize that laxity in the enforcement of consequences in school will leave a student unprepared for the workplace and for adult responsibilities. If you fail to do your work in a satisfactory manner, you get fired! We must ask, "What is the child learning when there are no consequences for clearly inappropriate actions?" Perhaps the child is learning that his violation of basic norms of civility has no consequences. This is clearly unacceptable. How can a school function and the members of a school flourish if there is a loss of civility within the life of the school? The school's role is to expect and reinforce accountability and civility. We must work with students to help them develop habits of civility, honor rules that focus on issues of social and physical safety and face the consequences if their actions violate accepted standards of behavior.

What is the child learning when there are no consequences for clearly inappropriate actions?

Let's say a student curses at and threatens a teacher. This is a serious offense that calls for immediate consequences. However, our consequences should be determined by a recognition of the student's choice and demonstration of a willingness to share power and respect with school authorities. Students who seem to welcome power struggles with authorities (for whatever reason) may not respond to the same set of consequences as a student who simply loses self-control. Students involved with serious power struggles need special interventions that often require time outside of the classroom. While discipline strategies to improve school civility can help students with power conflicts, the students must first agree to cede power to those administering the consequences. This is a discussion for another book, but we encourage the reader to study the works of others on this topic. (Goldstein, A. P., Harootunian, B., & Conoley, J. C. 1994. *Student aggression: Prevention, management, and replacement training*. New York: The Guilford Press; Meier, D. 1995. *The power of their ideas: Lessons for America from a small school in Harlem*. Boston: Beacon Press and Cohen, J. J., & Fish, M. C. 1993. *Handbook of school-based interventions: Resolving student problems and promoting healthy educational environments*. San Francisco: Jossey-Bass Publishers.)

For students who simply lose self-control, we can talk to them privately and discover what prompted the outburst. We can suggest ways to avoid this behavior in the future ("I understand you're angry that I won't extend your due date for your paper, but you may not speak to me in that manner. You could have said..."). Another consequence could be an immediate apology, preferably in front of the same people who witnessed the improper behavior, "You will apologize to me and to the rest of the class for your language now, and you will see me after class." If the student does not respond immediately, he/she should be sent to the next level of authority and receive some measured consequence. This may be a colleague across the hall that collaborates to provide a time-out location for student written reflection and appropriate response. We understand that there must be some consequences for the action, or we are telling that student—along with 25-30 other eagerly attentive peers—that cursing at a teacher is acceptable behavior.

Possible Consequences

Additional recommendations of consequences for serious violations of school civility come from Edward Wynne and Dr. Kevin Ryan in their book *Reclaiming Our Schools: A Handbook on Teaching Character, Academics, and Discipline*, 2nd Edition (1997). The authors stress the important role of consequences for students who choose to misbehave. They emphasize that effective punishments or consequences must have certain characteristics:

1. They must be clearly disliked by students—they must deter.
2. They must not absorb large amounts of school resources (e.g., schools cannot afford to assign a full-time paid adult monitor for each disobedient pupil).
3. They must be capable of being applied in "doses" of increasing severity.
4. They must not be perceived as cruel.
5. In public schools, they often must be applicable without strong cooperation from the parent of the pupil involved.
6. They must be able to be applied quickly—the next day, or even within one minute of the infraction, instead of the next week (p. 98).

Wynne and Ryan provide a long list of effective punishments or consequences for more serious violations. Some are listed below:

1. Subjecting pupils to before- or after-school detention within 24 hours of their violation (or, as one school found, Saturday detentions for more serious offenses, since they interrupted student's Saturday games and jobs).
2. Providing an in-school suspension in a designated room, supervised by a stern monitor, with chitchat prohibited and students assigned to do their missed class work.
3. Sharply and suddenly (and sometimes publicly) criticizing individual pupils for particular acts of misconduct, such as treating another student harshly.
4. Having erring pupils write notes to their parents explaining their misconduct, and having them promptly return the notes signed by their parents.
5. Calling the police immediately whenever any student conduct violates criminal law (p. 100).

Educators may reasonably maintain that a student who continually challenges school rules is begging for help. If this is so, the school staff should assist the student by providing counseling and support. While providing support to the student, school staff must also insist that this student exhibit the civil practices of the school and classroom or face consequences. If a student continually refuses to follow the practices established in school, there should be a measured consequence that helps the student reflect on his or her behavior, complete some act of reconciliation or restoration, and serve as a deterrent for future behavior. The key word here is *chooses*.

The majority of students know what they are doing and choose to do it, even those students we consider to be "emotionally handicapped." An atypical situation might be if a severely handicapped child, whose abilities to make decisions may be compromised, contributes to various interruptions. Our experiences with grades K-12 have exposed us to educators who have modeled and developed caring, learning environments with almost any kind of child in their classes—no matter what the child's classification. Civility can be modeled, taught and learned by almost any child within a normal classroom environment.

The Need for Consistency

We send a terrible message to students if consequences are not being applied in a consistent, fair manner. The failure to develop and enforce consequences is especially detrimental at the high school and middle school levels. At this age, students are developing a sense of right and wrong that involves the use of practices as beneficial in promoting a sense of a common good for themselves, their peers, and society at large. Students are constantly looking for order and fairness in their lives and how they and others are treated in relation to principles of fairness. They will also spot inequities as if they were blinking neon roadway signs. The following example addresses the issue of consistency:

Football is very important for the students and the community at Main High School. A senior player on the football team, Will, broke a school rule involving skipping class, which earned him a one-day suspension. Unfortunately, he broke this rule on a Friday, and since he was suspended that day (actually any suspension during a week results in a suspension for the remainder of that week's after-school activities), he could not participate in that night's football game. This was especially difficult since it was homecoming, but he knew what would happen if he broke the rule.

Several weeks later during the league championship games, Tom, the quarterback, was caught skipping class. The principal decided to hold off the suspension until Monday and allow Tom to quarterback for the team on Friday. Since they did not play the following week, the team would not be hurt.

Word about the principal's decision seeped out to the students, who became angry about the unfair treatment. Many students recognized the decision was made to win the football game, but it failed any reasonable standard of fairness. To their way of thinking, if Will had been suspended for the same offense, Tom should also be suspended on Friday and kept out of the game.

The students at Main High School "learned" from the principal's handling of this incident that who you are determines how you will be treated. If we truly want a "level playing field" for all students, then we have to make every effort to be as consistent as possible. The students took their case to the community and eventually the school board. They spoke of fairness and modeling of consistency. By not being consistent, the principal lost the respect of the students and much of the faculty. He resigned at the end of the year. If cutting class results in a one-day suspension, then the consequence must be enforced consistently.

This issue of consistency is not just an administrative problem. It extends to adults throughout the school. Elementary teachers face special issues with students who are in the halls all day, going to lunch, foreign language classes, P.E., music, art, special education, etc. Students need to know that any teacher, teacher's assistant, custodian, librarian, office staff member, or administrator may remind the disrespectful child of the need to return to civil practices within the school. These same adults can also praise or recognize students who are exhibiting  habits of civility. Consistent modeling, teaching, and reinforcement of civil practices by all adults will help children develop habits of civility. Young students who are unable to follow the practices in the beginning may need additional opportunities to develop the habits that will enable them to be successful. However, if some continue to disrupt the classroom environment, appropriate consequences should occur. Many primary teachers have found that the consequence of not allowing children time to play at recess, using this time instead as a time-out to talk about and revisit practices that promote greater civility, is a powerful tool to encourage better behavior and decision making. This consequence is not cruel, but it does make a powerful point. The child knows if he chooses to misbehave, he'll miss the fun.

Middle School Considerations

Middle schools similarly have special areas of concern because of the team framework in which they work. Teams can consist of two to five teachers who should try to develop consistent civil practices that are used and followed by all team students and teachers. These practices may be school-wide, to include all elective, rotation or special teachers, but may also involve some practices that are team-specific. This helps to ensure consistency throughout the school day for the children and the staff. Generally speaking, the nature of the high school results in a student having between six and eight teachers a day unless a child is on a "four-block" schedule which will result in four teachers per day per semester. However the number of teachers in the academic day does not account for any extracurricular-activity teachers and coaches. High schools must work with the entire school staff and students to seek consistency in their expectations of civility in the environment.

From an administrative point of view, if one teacher in the middle school team has far more office referrals than other team members, most likely this teacher needs some assistance in becoming more congruent in modeling and teaching the established practices designed to promote civility. If it were a team problem, the number of office referrals would be the same for all team members. The same applies in a high school setting. If an administrator notes that one teacher makes a large amount of referrals and that the children referred are rarely referred by any other teacher, then one can deduce that the teacher may need some additional assistance.

Skilled educators know firsthand that practices designed to promote habits of civility may not go smoothly with all students. They are willing to use time, instruction, encouragement, and consequences for students who choose to disrupt the learning environment for others. The consequences can start with a gentle reminder to reconsider the present behavior and can escalate to working cooperatively with a colleague to have a student move to the colleague's room for a time-out as another step before sending the child to the office, which may result in a suspension. What is important is that the student knows the teachers and administrators care and are willing to assist him or her in maintaining good conduct and will follow through with consequences. Even students with behavioral problems are expected to achieve steady improvement from the beginning of school to the end of the year. In this safe environment, most students will make progress, even if their home lives are less than ideal. The classroom becomes a haven of stability. Using punishment/consequence is the last alternative, but it can and should be used. Whether it's one teacher at a time or school teams that are committed to providing a structured caring environment for their students, both have consistent school-wide practices they follow to engender warm learning environments.

A middle school principal told one of the authors that the efforts of his school teams were responsible for office referrals dropping from nearly ten per day to fewer than one per day over a five-year period. The teams worked hard to develop and model consistent school-wide civil practices that were designed to create and ensure a caring environment for the students and adults in the school. Students who chose to misbehave encountered some of their established consequences that flowed from less to more severe. They are listed below:

Proximity to the child and/or a gentle pat on the back. This is to remind the child of the practices of civility that have been established and discussed by all in the community. It is very gentle in nature.

A strong stare, or the so-called "evil eye!" This is a little more focused on the child. The glare sends a message that the behavior needs to stop, but does not involve any dialogue with the child.

A short talk at the child's desk. Both the child and other children in the class are aware that the recent incivility is resulting in a little one-on-one time with the child. This low-volume discussion may also occur as the child is leaving the class. The child is confronted with his uncivil behaviors and asked what could be done to eliminate them. The discussion is friendly but firm; the behavior needs to change. A teacher might also ask the child to write a paper telling how he would feel if other students treated him this way.

A discussion of the behavior in the hallway during class. The child is removed from the class. The discussion is low-key, but clear and firm in its expectations. Everyone in the class is aware that the behavior of the child is causing problems and that it is getting rather serious. The next step will involve a discussion with the parent(s).

Call home to the parent. This is a very serious conversation in which the parent's support is being solicited to help restore the child to a more civil level of behavior before the administration is involved.

The teachers hoped that the less intrusive intervention—the pat on the back, a gentle reminder, a stare, or even a phone call to the home—would help a child refocus on the civility expectations of the class. However, if the child continues to be uncivil, he or she must "face the team." A misbehaving student sits down with the team members for a meeting. This meeting is not done around other children and is done during the student's elective class and during the teachers' team planning time. The principal or guidance counselor may attend the conference and, hopefully, a parent who is also committed to the process. An elective teacher may attend and will get someone to cover her class.

The meeting to face the team consists of serious discussions with the student. It is not intended to be a pleasant conference. Its clinical function is to determine what action must be taken to help the child stop the present behavior and to restore a practice of civility to the child's behavior. The teachers are polite, unemotional, and very firm about their expectations. They encourage the child to talk and to share his or her viewpoint. An attempt is made to find out why the child is acting in such a manner as to require a meeting between the child and the educators in the building. They remind the student of the consequences that will occur, such as the suspension from athletics and extracurricular activities, and eventually the suspension from school, if disruptive behavior continues. They also help the child develop a plan of action that they and the child will sign. What is most beneficial is what occurs at the end of the meeting. Often these meetings are emotionally hard on the students, the staff, and the parents. At the conclusion of the meeting, all the adults seek to touch and make a positive personal comment to the child. The team is welcoming the child back to the community. In essence, the ending of the meeting is the beginning of the healing process. The school's data indicated that most students (over 80 percent) who face the team never needed to come back to a session and improve in their caring and civility toward others.

Logical Consequences: Putting It Back on the Offenders

Before behavior continues to escalate to greater and greater incivility, one should also establish consequences or opportunities that are designed to help the child reflect on the transgression and develop steps to eliminate the negative behavior. Indeed we believe it is possible to develop strategies that help avoid the need for consequences that are generally enforced by adult figures. One such strategy is to have students reflect on what they have done under the leadership of a caring teacher.

Dr. Thomas Lickona, noted character educator and director of The Center for the 4th and 5th R's (Respect and Responsibility) shared a story and a useful strategy at a conference in Canandaigua, New York. It seems that a young child had been calling another child in the classroom an unwelcome name. At the end of the week, the mother of the little boy who had been called the unwelcome name called the teacher and stated that her son did not want to go to school the next week. She told the teacher about the incident and the name-calling. The teacher confronted the offending child about the name-calling. She explained to the child the difference between a small physical hurt and an inside hurt. She explained that inside hurts can hurt much longer than some physical hurts. She explained that the little boy had an inside hurt and asked the offender what he could do to stop a practice that was resulting in the child's hurt. The offender decided to apologize and not say unwelcome names again to the child. By having the child reflect on the deed and internalize what he had done, the offender came up with the solution to avoid hurting the child again. Notice the teacher was the facilitator in this episode. She helped the child consider the implications of what he was doing and then develop a strategy to remove the hurt. This strategy should be in the domain of K-12 teachers. It is not always enough to require a child to figure out on his or her own what he/she should do in a

A caring teacher can often help a child work through a difficult issue or develop strategies to avoid inappropriate behavior.

particular situation. A caring teacher can often help a child work through a difficult issue or develop strategies to avoid inappropriate behavior in the future.

Another practice is to have a "make right" of a particular wrong. This allows the student to compensate for hurt or damage to another person. It's a way to put the poor choice and misbehavior in the past. One of the best examples of "making right a wrong" can be viewed in episode 101, entitled "Opie the Birdman" from

"The Andy Griffith Show." At the beginning of the story, Opie was warned by his father (Andy) to be very careful with his slingshot and not shoot at anything that could get hurt. But acting like millions of boys before him, Opie shot a rock and killed the mother bird. Andy decided not to give Opie a "whipping" and instead went to Opie's room and opened up the window so Opie could hear those baby birds calling for their mother. At this point Opie assumed responsibility for his action. He reared the three young birds, which became his restitution for accidentally killing their mother. As a result, Opie helped develop two traits that are necessary for becoming a civil person: respect for life and a responsibility for one's actions.

One of the authors, while a principal in a school in Alaska, had an interesting experience. A boy set off a fire sprinkler which caused a huge mess in the ceiling tiles and carpet. With the permission from the maintenance crew, the boy's father, who was a licensed contractor, and the boy worked most of the night to shampoo and dry-vac the carpet and replace the ceiling tiles damaged by the water. When the staff and students came back to school the next day you could not tell that there had been a huge mess from the day before. The principal added some more consequences for the action, but the boy, with the remarkable initiative of his father, restored the damage that would have taken the school days and hundreds, if not thousands, of dollars in materials and labor. It also did the boy some good. He won the respect of many teachers and was able to fit back into the school. He knew that he had done something stupid but that he had also restored his damage. This is consistent with the *Responsive Classroom's* philosophy that, if possible—"If you break it, you fix it, if you fail to meet a responsibility, you lose a privilege and if you harm a person, you seek to restore the relationship."

In *Restitution: Restructuring School Discipline* (1992), Diane Gossen argues that teachers should encourage children to seek solutions to problems that would normally demand teacher intervention or consequences. For example, a child wrongs another child. The teacher does not immediately punish the child. Instead, the child who committed the offense works to make things right with the offended child, as Opie made things right with the baby birds and his father. Some might refer to Opie having a "logical consequence for his action." A child who is capable of restituting another child must have several characteristics:

1. S/he must have a sense of right and wrong.
2. S/he must acknowledge that s/he did wrong to another.
3. S/he must be capable of developing and implementing a plan that will make the wrong right. This plan and action must be agreed upon by the offended and the teacher.

The benefit of using restitution is that the child chooses to right the wrong. "Making it right" is a responsibility placed on the child who must then determine, with the offended child and perhaps the teacher, the logical consequence for the misdeed. The use of reflection in restitution requires an apology from the child and "forgiveness" from the victim. A caring classroom and school will accept this and welcome the child back to the school family. After all a famous teacher once said, "Let he who is without faults cast the first stone!"

Reframing is an excellent strategy to use when confronted by an angry and persistent student who refuses to respond to an initial direction or engage in the current class process. Reframing is not condoning the misbehavior, but it is a way to help the student de-escalate her emotions, begin to think and then redirect her behavior. It puts the responsibility back on the student. Reframing works best when: 1. You open doors, not close them, 2. You lower stakes, not raise them, 3. You give the student choices, and 4. You

"If you break it, you fix it, if you fail to meet a responsibility, you lose a privilege and if you harm a person, you seek to restore the relationship."

allow time to focus on the elevating goals of civility. Following are nine examples adapted from Curwin and Mendler's book, *Discipline with Dignity* (1988), concerning what one might say when reframing a particular incident.

1. I didn't know you (felt, thought, believed that). I would like to discuss this with you later. Can we meet after class? I need your help to let the class get back to work and then we can talk.
2. Your opinion is important to me, but can we address this later? I would be happy to speak with you after this...
3. You might be right about that, however, this isn't the time to solve this problem, and can we meet...?
4. I'm glad you feel you can trust me to be so honest. I'm concerned about your opinion, but I need to keep this class running too. Can you help by meeting with me?
5. There's probably some truth in what you perceive. However, you sound pretty upset right now. I would like to help you, but could you first help us complete this class and then you and I can talk?
6. Well, obviously we disagree right now, but I am willing to listen, are you? Let's complete this class and then sit down and talk.
7. You must be pretty upset to say that here. I am willing to hear you out, but first you need to take some time to settle down. Would you help me by allowing this class to finish their work and then you and I can talk?
8. I want to hear your side of the story, but it cannot happen right now. Please help me by taking a break and then we can talk after class.
9. Well, I don't know if you meant to say it that way, but let's take a break here, let me finish this class and then we can talk.

Teachers can practice reframing by role-modeling their own response. Practice how you would respond to the following hypothetical classroom incidents: 1. A class clown, 2. A tattler, 3. A defiant student, 4. A chronically tardy student, 5. An angry student.

Several years ago, one of the authors attended a training conducted by "Educators for Social Responsibility." They have graciously given permission for the author to share with others the insights he garnered from this training concerning the use of "I" messages. The "I" message is a useful conflict resolution strategy to help an individual confront a problem in a civil manner. During any conflict, a person has the choice to: (1) fight for his/her own way, (2) give up and abandon a personal concern or desire, or (3) respectfully assert a concern and attempt to engage the other party in a constructive response. The "I" message can help assert a concern without attacking the other party. A person will choose to use an "I" message to show respect for the other party in a conflict, to avoid an escalation of conflict by not using attacking language and attempt to engage the other party by clearly noting the point of conflict and offering an alternative.

The traditional structure of an "I" message includes the following statements.

- "I feel (state your emotion),
- when you (state the specific behavior),
- because (state the effect the behavior has on your life),
- and I would like (state the specific behavior you would prefer to see.)"

A person using an "I" message is not attacking the other party, but puts the focus of concern on himself—the "I" in the message. Someone using an "I" message would not use put-downs or insults. The goal of the "I" message is to bring the other party to recognition of the concern and provide a reasonable alternative. As with the strategy of reframing, it opens a door to negotiation.

Practice is the key to helping the strategy become a natural response. Work with a colleague and practice with your own words using the structure of an "I" message to address the following potential conflicts.

1. You are noticing a student in your class continues to talk to other students when you are speaking.

I feel _____

when you _____

because_____

and I would like_____

2. Another staff member has borrowed things from you three or four times recently. He forgot to return the things to you the last two times. He has just asked to borrow something else.

I feel _____

when you _____

because _____

and I would like _____

3. Your supervisor has given you several new projects recently that are over and above your regular responsibilities. She has just asked you to take on another.

I feel _____

when you _____

because _____

and I would like _____

For further training on "I" messages contact Educators for Social Responsibility.

Students will need a similar introduction and scenarios to practice the skill of "I" messages. Research by the Educators for Social Responsibility has noted that any new skill requires multiple practice sessions (20-30 sessions) to become a natural part of someone's behavior. We encourage teachers to carefully select specific conflict resolution skills to teach and model as part of their overall goal to create a civil classroom.

Another excellent strategy that is gaining wider acceptance in schools is the use of a peer mediator. Elementary as well as middle and high school students throughout the country have been trained in facilitating mediation between students. In most peer mediation efforts, a third party comes together with the two protagonists and seeks to "work out" the dispute. Nucci (2001) cites the benefits of utilizing peer mediation:

First and foremost, the act of peer mediation reduces the tendency for students to see objections to immoral conduct as simply a matter of adult authority. Second, it causes the disputants to see their situation from a third disinterested vantage point. This third-person perspective moves the issue out of one of direct reciprocity, offering a window into a new way of looking at moral issues. Finally, it is of benefit to the mediator who is necessarily engaged in moral discourse and reflection (p.157).

Finally we can consider the use of time-out for students who momentarily lose self-control. Generally time-out is used at the preschool through primary grades. A child is removed from a particular event and is asked to reflect on what she did wrong. When ready, the child may come to the teacher and talk about the transgression as well as what she should do to rejoin the group. Perhaps the teacher may have a child that was offended join the conversation. The goal is to restore civility to the relationships. There are other ways to use time-outs that can be very productive for older students—especially students who are behaviorally challenged or easily angered by comments from teachers or students that would not anger other students in the classroom (e.g., a student disagrees with what a peer said regarding her interpretation of literature). The "aggrieved" lashes out with anger aimed at the child who was making a legitimate point. Students with control issues can be taught to time themselves out or leave the classroom and stand outside the classroom door, without teacher intervention, if they are beginning to feel anger or hostility toward a teacher or others in the classroom. Here the child can take some deep breaths and seek to calm down. Afterward, the child can try to determine what is causing him to get upset and decide what he needs to do to ensure that his behavior does not cause any further disruptions within the class. When the child feels that he can rejoin the group, he comes back into the classroom. He may need to talk to the teacher, or he may feel comfortable returning to his seat. Based on the situation, the teacher could seek a conversation with the child during or right after the class to see if the problem has been resolved. At this point, if there are still issues that could impede on the civil nature of the class, the teacher might seek further dialogue with the child or have the child and other students meet to work out their problems. What is important is that the child is assuming responsibility for his actions. Several teachers noted to the author that teaching students coping and behavioral strategies with the option of self "timing out" helped some children avoid consequences that were directed by a teacher or administration.

We have provided several different approaches to consequences. Some are more dependent on teachers while others are more dependent on having students "right a wrong." You may prefer strategies from the Wynne and Ryan selection for more serious and grievous acts and favor the use of time-out, or Gossen's restitution approach to consequences for inappropriate behavior that is not seriously disruptive. Perhaps you want to be more proactive rather than reactive in your thinking about conse-quences. But isn't it unconscionable to allow students to act inappropriately time after time, when practicing civil traits such as courtesy, respect, and responsibility along with develop-ing insights and strategies regarding their behaviors will help them in their lives? If modeling, practicing, teacher dialoguing, reflection and peer pressure don't work, then consequences must be utilized.

If modeling, practicing, teacher dialoguing, reflection and peer pressure don't work, then consequences must be utilized.

This doesn't mean that we shouldn't con-sider the circumstances resulting in a child's misconduct. A child who is going through a rough time may need extra attention and acknowledgment of his or her difficulties. Staff should be made aware of these situations, and extra help afforded in suggesting more appropriate behavior. Peer helpers can be enlisted to spend additional time with the child. Our main thrust is assisting all students and providing them with nurturing envi-ronments from which to learn. Still, consequences for inappropriate behavior must be considered and applied.

In conclusion, the effort to achieve civility in a school by establishment of civil practices will only be as effective as the effort to enforce consequences for those who *continually choose* to flout the rules that establish boundaries for acceptable behavior.

Therefore, we must be prepared to enforce consequences. We must also assess the climate of the class to determine if it is an inviting one for students and adults. Is the classroom one of civility toward all? Do teachers and students work together to develop a civil, caring environment? Is there a genuine love between the teacher and the students? It is impossible to like every child we teach, but we should seek to love every child we teach. Notice the difference. If we simply like children, we can excuse poor behavior, just as we excuse poor behavior of some friends. But if we love students, we must help them do the right thing by modeling, talking, sharing, encouraging, and, if necessary, enforcing consequences.

If we love students, we must help them do the right thing.

As Aristotle noted, habits of civility are the building blocks for the formation of the virtuous and/or civil person. However, to stop here would leave us only partially finished with our mission. We must also develop in children the intellectual understanding of why civility is so important. The next part of our work will address how the use of the curriculum can help shape the intellectual aspect of civility.

CHAPTER 6

Promoting Civility through the Curriculum

with Paul Weimer

L et us return to the introduction and reexamine the meaning of the word *civilized*.

> **ADJECTIVE: 1. Having a highly developed** society and culture. 2. Showing evidence of moral and intellectual advancement; humane, ethical, and reasonable. 3. Marked by refinement in taste and manners; cultured; polished.

Consider the first and third definitions. Hopefully, we live in a highly developed society and culture. We have a sense of taste and good manners. We admire people who are cultured and polished in how they handle themselves in various situations. However we are incomplete in our understanding of the word *civilized* unless we consider the second definition: "Showing evidence of moral and intellectual advancement; humane, ethical, and reasonable." It suggests tying together reasoning and ethics with moral and intellectual advancement. A civil person is one who possesses more than courtesies. A civil person is also one who is morally and ethically accountable and sound in her practices. A civil person uses his intellect to seek humane and reasonable explanations and solutions to perplexing moral problems. Simply put, a civilized person is educated and capable of understanding the moral and social requirements of citizenship in a home, community, nation, and the world. Obviously, this training begins in the home, but it must also be a focal point of the school. In developing the civil child, one must acknowledge the role that climate both in the home and the school must play. However, school also consists of curriculum and we must acknowledge and focus on the curriculum as a tool to foster moral and intellectual advancement. We are, in essence, reconnecting with Aristotle. Aristotle reminds us of the importance that habits must play in the development of the civil child as well as the civil school. We need common practices, like being respectful, responsible and caring, that are used to foster a civil environment. But to stop here, we will fail to educate the intellectual side of the moral and civil child. We must also develop the intellect. In this sense, we are uniting the habits with the intellect in developing the civil person. This chapter will focus on how this can be done. We will provide examples and hopefully offer some strategies that can help us mine the curriculum for examples and insights on living the civil life. Let us begin with John Donne's most famous quote: "No man is an island."

We Are Not Alone

In his *Meditation XVII*, John Donne offers a profound reflection on the interconnection of lives, noting that when one person is diminished, so are all of us. Likening each of us to a part of the very earth of a continent, he notes that the loss of a single part has an impact upon the shape of the rest. With civility, we are working with a concept that explicitly acknowledges the connection of members of society, and for our purposes, the school society. However, as in all efforts in education, we are seeking to grow citizens into the larger role they all must play.

A starting point is to acknowledge that there is a fundamental reason why we are educators. We have chosen to act as transmitters of knowledge from one generation to the next. We model and instruct; we impart skills, we train, we lead, and we help children learn to reason. We prepare our students for community life, the job force, or for the next level of learning. We provide and teach them to use intellectual tools we have mastered for them to make their own and to use in life. They are tools that have been handed

There is a fundamental reason why we are educators. We have chosen to act as transmitters of knowledge from one generation to the next.

down to us, linking us with generations who have come and gone before us.

With these tools our students achieve new vistas and insights, gaining perspective on the wide world of what could have been or what might yet be, inspired to new thought and new endeavors to create a better and more civil life. Through our work as educators, the fabric of civilization, of civility, is sustained. The heart of the curriculum, the part that is quantifiable, is where we play a role in "intellectual advancement" per the definition noted above. The qualities of moral advancement, the humane, ethical and reasonable capacities in our definition come both from the expectations of behavior we establish and also from the inspiration that can be sparked through the very topics we teach. Let's now consider how both of these aspects of civility are addressed at the same time.

Working Through the Curriculum

The humanities subject areas are among the richest areas for helping young people appreciate how we are all linked as members of a community and as members of a larger society. When we speak of the humanities, we are talking of a wide range of subject areas, many of them not independently studied in the K-12 curriculum, but represented in countless ways.

What are the humanities? As defined by the 1965 National Foundation on the Arts and the Humanities Act, the federal law that established the National Endowment for the Humanities:

> **The term "humanities" includes,** but is not limited to, the study of the following: language, both modern and classical; linguistics; literature; history; jurisprudence; philosophy; archaeology; comparative religion; ethics; the history, criticism and theory of the arts; those aspects of social sciences which have humanistic content and employ humanistic methods; and the study and application of the humanities to the human environment with particular attention to reflecting our diverse heritage, traditions, and history and to the relevance of the humanities to the current conditions of national life.

It's a long list! But it surely does represent fruitful areas for exploring and inspiring the kinds of behaviors that comprise civility. Let's consider some examples of how these subject areas enter the classroom and the life of the school.

As a core subject area in K-12 education, social studies has come to be the place where a range of independent subjects converge: history, geography, economics, civics, government, biography, and more, with many of these thematically integrated

in units in the early elementary years. For example, consider how primary educator's exercises on "your family" or "your community" may function to sow the seeds of civility as we have outlined it. Learning family history may help young people to begin to appreciate how individuals who are known to them have contributed to their life. By extension, knowledge of community history becomes a way for students to begin to understand the interplay of their individual life story with a larger one, the life of the community, and beyond that, the life of a nation. Simple timelines are an often-used strategy, and can include events ranging from the advent of the local mall or fast food or video store to the major historical markers that have come to define community heritage. With these lessons, it is not hard to introduce the locally relevant details that touch on economics, government, and the individual life stories of people who have made a difference. In all of them, recurring themes and questions help to stimulate thinking about civility: what behaviors made it possible for this person (business) to be a success? What behaviors have made it possible for this community to live as neighbors? Have there been particular rules (laws) that have been necessary to provide for the well being of the community? Are there particular rules in your family that help you get along?

Georgia on Our Minds

In the local setting, community history is often represented in a local museum or historical society, and sometimes by a long-standing business, be it a bank, a bakery, or a farm. It is hard to replicate in the classroom the kinds of learning experiences that can come from off-campus trips to institutions and organizations that understand your lesson goals. For example, museums large and small often employ volunteers who might have some personal knowledge of events or themes represented in the organization—the "living history" aspect of that kind of history can truly bring home an appreciation of themes in civility. A powerful example of this can be found in the Mighty Eighth Air Force Museum in Savannah, Georgia. There, veterans of WWII serve as guides to the exhibits and share their own real-life experiences to students. First-person narrative of our history, whether it was acted out in the local community or on a larger stage, helps bring events to life in a way that few books can.

In another outstanding exercise in community history, master teacher Sandra Worsham of Milledgeville, Georgia, chose to hone her high school students' writing skills through oral history projects. Funded by a grant from a local foundation, Worsham helped her students learn basic oral history techniques and set them to the task of gathering the rich life stories and experiences of the elders in their community. Working with journals and tapes, the students shared the stories in class and worked on transcribing them. Not surprisingly, the personal contact involved in gathering the stories led the students to feel a personal investment in seeing to it that each was carefully recorded and refined for sharing. Eventually published as *Everybody Has a Story to Tell: Stories of Flannery O'Connor's Milledgeville*, the project not only served to develop writing skills in writing-challenged students, it also served to foster an appreciation for, and a heightened sense of community, in both students and the local citizenry.

Hands-on historical learning is a powerful way to help young people place themselves in a continuum of civility.

Hands-on historical learning is another powerful way to help young people place themselves in a continuum of civility. In the North Fulton County Teaching Museum in Roswell, Georgia (a suburb of Atlanta), students are invited to re-enact landmark decisions of the U.S. Supreme Court. In a replica courtroom, students have an opportunity to dress as justices and present (and hear) historical cases. Pre-visit and post-visit curricula emphasize not only the nature of the social issue of the case, but also the system of laws that makes it possible for deeply divisive issues to be addressed in American law. The big questions addressed in the Supreme Court can usually be translated to issues that can be introduced to students across grade levels, addressing fundamental issues of fairness. Helping young people start to think about these issues helps to form the idea of a much bigger world beyond the classroom.

As suggested in the example of Milledgeville above, studying history and the forces at work in daily life are also exercises in learning individual history or biography. It is hard to imagine an easier way to engage young people in the wider world than to help them understand it through the lives of historical actors, both large and small. We all know the pleasure of mastery, of personal investment in an issue that comes from researching and learning the role that an individual has played in an historical event, be it the challenges met and risks taken by an inventor or explorer, or the courage and leadership of a great politician or social reformer. A wonderful Internet resource developed in Macon, Georgia, *www.characterworks.com*, offers a superb example: each day a very brief profile marking the anniversary of daily landmarks in history and biography highlights a particular trait characterized by an individual's life or achievement. Sample quotations further stimulate discussion of the behaviors that characterized the achievement, and brief suggestions for activities or discussion prompt contemporary reflection and action on the relevance of the achievement or trait in daily life. Characterworks.com is an outstanding reminder that every day presents an opportunity to bring history, literature, and a wide range of other subject areas into the focus of the overall curriculum with a timeliness and relevance that serve to cement an appreciation for the achievements that come through our life in community.

Literature and the Arts

While the social studies curriculum helps introduce concepts of civility in the world as we understand it, literature and the arts present opportunities to explore visions of the world through the eyes of creative minds through the ages. Great works in literature and drama engage in timeless questions of what constitutes the good life, of a life well lived. Outstanding moral questions that have stimulated discussion and debate through the ages are played out, and sweeping visions of the human condition are explored. Consider the rich opportunities for addressing contemporary issues of community and personal responsibility in playwrights ranging from Sophocles and Shakespeare to Henrik Ibsen and Arthur

Great works in literature and drama engage in timeless questions of what constitutes the good life, of a life well lived.

Miller. The prospects for discussion of great drama and literary classics are endless for the simple reason that they have *become* classics because of their enduring ability to engage us in thought and discussion that transcend the limits of the period in which they were created; they continue to speak to us on issues that are relevant to our lives as individuals and members of a community.

Similarly, the fine arts, including music and art history, are revealing of forces in our lives that cut across time and place. Why does the enigmatic smile of the Mona Lisa continue to captivate? How is it that we continue to admire the physical ideals represented in ancient Greek and Roman sculpture? Why does Pachelbel's *Canon in D* speak to us as a stately progression, Bach's *Toccata and Fugue in D Minor* as majestic and imposing, or Beethoven's symphonies as narrative visions? We can also use contemporary music. Right after 9/11, folksinger Tom Paxton composed a moving piece, *The Bravest*. Following are some of the lyrics:

The first plane hit the other tower
Right after I came in
It left a gaping, fiery hole
Where offices had been.
We stood and watched in horror
As we saw the first ones fall
Then someone yelled, "Get out! Get out!
They're trying to kill us all."

I grabbed the pictures from my desk
And joined the flight for life.
With every step I called the names
Of my children and my wife.
And then we heard them coming up
From several floors below.
A crowd of fire fighters,
With their heavy gear in tow.

CHORUS:
Now every time I try to sleep
I'm haunted by the sound
Of firemen pounding up the stairs
While we were coming down.

And when we met them on the stairs
They said we were too slow.
"Get out! Get out!" they yelled at us—
"The whole thing's going to go."
They didn't have to tell us twice—
We'd seen the world on fire.
We kept on running down the stairs
While they kept climbing higher.

We could use this piece for a discussion of how we felt on 9/11. We could try to place ourselves in the position of the firemen during this day. Did they know they were placing themselves in harm's way? Why would they choose to do this? What might they have been thinking about their families? What type of person would choose to be a fireman? This is but one example of the use of music to awaken in us the quality of the lives of those around us. There are countless prompts for stimulating a wider view of the world around us in the arts.

Exploring great themes in the human experience through the arts can be inspiring and life-changing. This recognition is at the heart of the Bernstein Model of enriching the curriculum through the arts. Beginning by studying a masterwork of drama, literature or music in the classroom, the method progresses through the process of coming to understand the work intellectually to the challenge of staging and performing the work for an audience. Culminating performances often feature additional programming that provide opportunities for students to further share their appreciation and understanding of the issues treated in the work.

Considering Great Ideas

Clearly we value the exposure and work of children and adults in exploring and analyzing how civility can be developed through our school curriculum. Let us consider how research informs us of strategies we may use to facilitate intellectual and civil awareness of children and adults. Civil awareness can help facilitate the establishment of a civil school and, hopefully, a civil community and nation. Let us consider the following excerpts from famous texts.

We the people of the United States, in order to form a more perfect union, establish justice, insure domestic tranquility, provide for the common defense, promote the general welfare, and secure the blessings of liberty to ourselves and our posterity, do ordain and establish this Constitution for the United States of America.

Preamble to the Constitution of the United States

Four score and seven years ago, our fathers brought forth on this continent a new nation conceived in liberty and dedicated to the proposition that all men are created equal.

Now we are engaged in a great civil war, testing whether that nation or any nation so conceived and so dedicated, can long endure. We are met on a great battlefield of that war. We have come to dedicate a portion of that field as a final resting place for those who here gave their lives that that nation might live. It is altogether fitting and proper that we should do this....

Abraham Lincoln, Gettysburg Address

A just law is a man-made code that squares with the moral law or the law of God. An unjust law is a code that is out of harmony with the moral law. To put it in the terms of Saint Thomas Aquinas, an unjust law is a human law that is not rooted in eternal and natural law. Any law that uplifts human personality is just. Any law that degrades human personality is unjust.

Dr. Martin Luther King, Jr., Letter from a Birmingham Jail

Love of honor is the only feeling that does not grow old. And the last pleasure when one is weak with age is not, as some say, making money, but having the respect of our fellow men.

Pericles, From the Funeral Speech

Those who are materially poor can be very wonderful people. One evening we went out and we picked up four people from the street. And one of them was in a most terrible condition. I told the Sisters: "You take care of the other three; I will take care of the one who looks worse." So I did for her all that my love can do. I put her in bed, and there was such a beautiful smile on her face. She took hold of my hand, as she said one word only: "thank you"—and she died. I could not help but examine my conscience before her. And I asked: "What would I say if I were in her place?" And my answer was very simple. I would have tried to draw a little attention to myself. I would have said: "I am hungry, I am dying, I am cold, I am in pain," or something. But she gave me much more—she gave me her grateful love. And she died with a smile on her face.

Excerpt from a speech of Mother Teresa

And finally the following parable taken from Tolstoy and put in this story form by Christina Hoff Sommers:

There was once a rabbi in a small Jewish village in Russia who vanished every Friday morning for several hours. The devoted villagers boasted that during these hours their rabbi ascended to heaven to talk with God. A skeptical newcomer arrived in town, determined to discover where the rabbi really was.

One Friday morning the newcomer hid near the rabbi's house and watched him rise, say his prayers and put on the clothes of a peasant. He saw him take an axe and go into the forest, chop down a tree and gather up a large bundle of wood. Next, the rabbi proceeded to a shack in the poorest section of the village in which lived an old woman and her sick son. He left them the wood, which was enough for a week. The rabbi then quietly returned to his own house.

The story concludes that the newcomer stayed on in the village and became a disciple of the rabbi. And when he hears one of his fellow villagers say, "On Friday morning our rabbi ascends all the way to heaven," the newcomer quietly adds, "If not higher."

Each of the previous excerpts address issues of civility and the moral and social obligations we have toward others. Pericles reminds us that achieving the respect of our neighbors and friends is our true legacy. King reminds us that there can be a difference between laws that degrade human personality and those that uplift human personality. The Preamble instructs the citizens of the United States of their obligations as "we the people." Lincoln's Gettysburg Address has many powerful points of civility, not the least of which is the equal worth of all human beings. Mother Teresa points out the wonderful dignity that the poorest among us might possess. The rabbi is just a little better, a little kinder than most of us. As adults we can recognize the wonderful example of kindness the rabbi illustrates. We can admire the rabbi for not calling attention to his actions. He cut and gathered the wood because a neighbor needed help. We can see rabbi as a moral compass, but our children may not. Our children, whether they are elementary, middle, or high school students, may not see a moral or social message in any of the above passages, nor see the moral meaning within the passage that the author or the teachers *hoped* the students would recognize. Indeed, research proves to us that we would be wrongheaded to make the assumption that students see and understand what we see and understand from a reading selection.

What Do We Learn From Readings?

Dr. Darcia Narvaez from Notre Dame University is one of the foremost researchers and writers in the area of social and moral development. Over the last few years she and some of her colleagues have turned their efforts to determining what children learn by reading moral stories and, in particular, if they grasp the moral messages within the stories. In Narvaez, Bentley, Gleason, and Samuels (1998) and Narvaez, Gleason, Mitchell, and Bentley (1999) the researchers noted that the developmental level of third grade, fifth grade and college students was a greater predictor than reading comprehension as to whether they "got" the moral meaning of a story. In the second study the researchers determined that:

> **...the younger children were much less likely** to select the correct theme (11% of the time across stories); the older children selected the theme about half the time (45%); and the adults selected the theme nearly all of the time (91%). When selections and ratings were combined into an overall "the comprehension score" and reading comprehension was covaried out, developmental differences were large (effect size=1.00). In summary, children do not necessarily understand the theme of a story as intended by the author. Although many children will generate or select a theme when asked, the selection is often "wrong" according to an adult or author perspective (p. 6).

Just because a child reads a moral story doesn't mean the child will understand the moral message contained within the story. The child applies his/her experiences and scheme of understanding to the story. Now one could argue that the job of the teacher would be to help "clarify" the story's intent to the child. Yet this might be more difficult than first thought. Narvaez (2002) notes:

> **Think about seeing a movie like *Pulp Fiction*.** Say that you believe the theme to be one of glorifying violence and disregard for human life. But your companion finds it to be an avant-garde work that cleverly depicts realistic, smart people gone wrong—as we all could. Do you change your mind about the message? ...When you watched the film, you assimilated a theme based on your prior knowledge and experience, but in discussing the theme with your companion you are able to accommodate your thinking about the film to include your friend's viewpoint.

What happens in the case of a child? A child has a certain intuition about the message of a story but then an adult suggest that he or she is wrong and that this other message is the "right one." What does the child do? (This is an empirical question—but it is theoretically answerable.) The child might nod, and maybe even mouth the message, if old enough. But the child is very likely unable to take the perspective of the adult and blend it with his or her own as you did.... (pp. 164-65).

> Simply put, a child's intellectual, as well as his moral and social, development may not allow him to truly understand what the adult is saying or, for our purposes, what the child is reading. The child is unable to fit the new information into his experiences. He does not have enough *schemas*—"those generalized knowledge structures that you have built from experience." A child's conception of justice may be and probably is different from an adult's. A child's conception of fairness may be different. Experience and the gradual intellectual growth of the child will allow the child to develop increasingly complex schemes to process ideas and information.

> Of course the next question is whether children can be taught to extract the author's moral theme contained within narratives or stories. Narvaez (2001), citing the work of her colleagues (Narvaez, Mitchell, Endicott, & Bock, 1999), determined some strategies one can use to enhance a child's understanding of the moral and social implications contained within literature and narratives.

1. Be aware that some demands are in conflict with apparent demands (e.g., personal/inner, outer/social). This may be studied by discussing: What was the problem? What was the worst thing the character faced? Were there differences in what people wanted? What were the differences?

2. Increase students' moral sensitivity to the configuration of the situation. This may be accomplished by asking these questions: What was going on? Who was thinking about what was going on? Who could be affected? Who was affected?

3. Help students reason about possible actions (moral sensitivity and reasoning), by posing questions such as: What could be done? What would happen if ___? What outcomes might occur? How might people react?

4. Focus students' attention on their own, as well as characters' personal identities and moral motivation, with questions like: What did the character think about when deciding/doing the deed? What kind of ideals were driving the character in the story?

5. Increase students' awareness of sacrifice or sublimation of personal gratification for a greater good (moral motivation). Ask: How did the action affect each character in the story? How did the action affect the community (e.g., classroom, neighborhood)?

6. Help students notice follow through: How did the character carry out the action? Where there were obstacles, what did the character do?

7. Develop students' skills in interpreting the social outcome and implicit or explicit positive judgment of action taken: How did the story end—good or bad? Why? For whom was it a good ending? For whom was it a bad ending?

8. Develop students' skills in reflecting on alternative endings: How could the outcome have turned out better for everyone? (pp. 164-165).

In conclusion, Narvaez and her colleagues have done the most thorough research on whether moral stories can facilitate the character and, we hope, the civil development of children. She recognizes that children, as well as adults, use prior knowledge when assessing the meaning from a reading. In other words, we try to make sense of what we are reading based on what we have previously read or experienced. This is why a story about the procedures needed to board an airplane would make greater sense and have greater meaning to someone who has flown several times compared to someone who has never been to an airport or flown on an airplane. This doesn't mean that one does not learn when reading information or ideas that are foreign or different. It does mean that the more comfortable one is with the topic, the easier the assimilation of the material into one's intellectual understandings or schema. Those who have taught school have seen this happen over and over as some children struggle with the meaning of texts while others quickly assess the meaning or intent of a particular reading.

Narvaez has thrown down a powerful challenge. Her research indicates that we are not passive readers, that we as readers bring our experiences and abilities to the text. For example, the authors are much more comfortable reading from the humanities or education writings than physics. We lack the schemes and background understanding to understand physics unless we are reading a physics book written for the general public. We hope that children will understand the moral messages in stories, but there is no guarantee this will happen. There are background considerations that influence whether one "gets the message." For example, taking middle or high school students to see *West Side Story* may result in some students who focus on the moral themes in the play while other fail to see them due to a focus on the justification for the gang warfare. Whether one is in a gang may taint one's perspective of the moral message. Clearly, we as educators have a difficult job, but there are strategies that could be most beneficial.

Facilitating Moral Understanding

We must become active participants with the students in thinking, reading, and processing the curriculum. Since research has determined that children will often simply not "get it," then we must help students develop a deeper understanding of the moral and social issues within a reading or a piece of art. We will need to re-think our pedagogical approach in order to facilitate thinking, experiencing, and reasoning about the moral and social ideas contained within the humanities. The *Paideia* method may be a good place to help us organize our pedagogical approach. The *Paideia* method utilizes seminars or good conversations as a tool to enhance a child's understanding of a text. The seminar also requires basic civilities of listening and responding to the ideas of others with respect and courtesy. In the book *The Power of Paideia Schools* (1998), Terry Roberts describes a seminar as...

A formal discussion based on a text in which the leader asks only open-ended questions. Text in this instance can have widely varied meanings: artwork, music, photographs, video, maps, a math or science problem, and facsimiles of historical documents, as well as more traditional texts. For a seminar to be effective, however, the group must be able to focus on a common item in order to prevent the formal discussion from disintegrating into a bull session. Within the context of this discussion, students are required to study the text carefully, listen closely to the comments of others, think critically for themselves, and articulate both their own thoughts and their responses to the thoughts of others. From the students' point of view, the seminar differs from most other formal classroom experiences in that it asks them to voice and examine their own thinking at a sophisticated level, not replay the thoughts of teacher or textbook.... The seminar leader will ask them [the students] to think about evocative values and ideas throughout—examining, defending and clarifying their own ideas and those of others. Many seminar leaders also have students write more or less formal statements not only before and after the seminar but also during the seminar itself as a way of enhancing their thinking (pp. 12-13).

The seminar is not the initial step in the learning process. It is the final step in helping students improve their understanding of the ideas within a curricular offering. A good seminar experience will demand preparation on the part of the teacher as well as the student. Mortimer Adler (1982, 1983, 1984) advocated the use of seminar in education through his "Paideia Proposal." Briefly, the Paideia Proposal utilizes three schemes of learning—the first two schemes as preparation for the seminar. The first is *didactic instruction*, or the acquisition of knowledge by direct instruction, features lectures and factual recall of information. This is a good place to make use of graphic organizers or outlines to assist students in understanding the information. The second scheme involves the development of *intellectual skills* or *skills of learning*. One would work to improve reading, writing, listening, and thinking skills.

We must become active participants with the students in thinking, reading, and processing the curriculum.

This might include the development of thinking skills such as sequencing, comparing and contrasting, and the application of these skills to learning opportunities in the classroom and community. For example, students could consider through biography those who chose a life of service to others. Then the student(s) might organize and engage in service activities in the school and community to gain a greater understanding of the value and call of service to others. It is at this step that the student applies his learning and gains a greater understanding than simply factual recall. The National Paideia Center recommends that 10-15 percent of the time be spent in didactic exercises, 60-70 percent be spent in the development of intellectual skills, and 15-20 percent be spent in the seminar as a way to increase the understanding of ideas and concepts developed in the second step of learning. The seminar, conversation, is the culmination. The seminar as a "great conversation" demands the intellectual and social skills of students.

Wanda H. Ball and Pam Brewer, in their book *Socratic Seminars in the Block* (2000), illustrate the differences between a seminar discussion and a typical classroom discussion. Notice how the seminar discussions demand greater attention and involvement on the part of the students than a typically teacher-led discussion.

Socratic Seminars

- Students and teachers are in a circle. All have eye contact: teacher is on the same level.
- 97 percent student talk; students know teachers won't comment.
- Average response for students is 8-12 seconds.
- No verbal or non-verbal approval is present. Affirming feedback by the teacher is taboo.
- Thinking, backed up with textual evidence is paramount. Open-ended exploration, not rightness, is valued.
- Students listen primarily to peers.
- Students have ownership for most of the flow.
- Students are held accountable for contributions based upon criteria that have been agreed upon.

Class Discussions

- Students are often in rows. Teacher is set apart and often higher on a stool or behind a podium.
- 97 percent teacher talk, even if many questions are asked. Teacher elaborates and answers.
- Average response for students is 2-3 seconds.
- Teacher affirmation of correctness is typical. Sustaining feedback for incorrectness is expected.
- Rightness is usually paramount; thinking ends as soon as someone is right.
- Students listen primarily to the teacher, who has the answer
- Teachers have ownership for most of the flow.
- Students see discussion as a frill, a nebulous negligible "participation grade." If you miss class, you didn't miss much (p. 11).

The seminar is truly a "great conversation" in which the input and ideas of others are debated within a climate of courtesy. Having a successful seminar demands habits of civility that hopefully students have or are learning. For example, students and adults must learn to listen to the reasoning and ideas of others. To be successful in this endeavor, students and teachers will need to model civility toward others. Ball and Brewer have noted some responsibilities for participants in a seminar. Some of their responsibilities are listed below:

- Giving my opinions clearly yet succinctly
- Disagreeing with the ideas of others, not with the people
- Clarifying information and lending support to a peer's argument
- Taking issue with inaccuracies or illogical reasoning
- Listening attentively and patiently as peers share their ideas
- Listening acutely to a peer's position before taking issue with it
- Maintaining an open mind to a diversity of opinions
- Exercising patience and self-control
- Being courteous and respectful of my peers
- Avoiding all side conversations
- Avoiding body language with negative connotations (pp. 13-14)

A seminar will not be successful unless all participants listen respectfully when considering the ideas of others, learn to disagree without being disagreeable, and accept that the "sacred" ideas that one might have before beginning a seminar can change through the interactive learning experience. A seminar is a time to examine one's ideas in a supportive and instructive environment. It encourages a greater understanding of powerful issues and ideas that shape our understanding of what it means to be human and, more important, what it means to be a human being with responsibilities toward others.

Learning to Ask Good Questions

In conclusion, utilizing a seminar approach to learning will require that the teachers as well as the students develop a basic understanding of the text, art or piece of music being considered. We will then need to analyze the work, applying our thinking and reasoning skills, looking for moral ideas, conflicts and issues that will require greater discussion and/or action. After we and the students enhance our  understanding of the material, we must engage our students in a "moral conversation." During a moral conversation, we have a discussion on the issues and ideas contained within a piece of literature, lyrics within a song, or an examination of a piece of music or a narrative. We should try to sit in a circle that will promote a more easy and natural discussion than sitting in rows or around tables. In essence our goal is to have a conversation focused on the ideas contained within the work we are considering. The conversation allows us to consider how others are contemplating the ideas contained within the work, to agree or disagree with their interpretations and, most important, to learn from each other. This will require that we, as conversation leaders and facilitators, maintain questioning strategies that will further the conversation. Some years ago after Lawrence Kohlberg (1958 & 1984) had formulated and described a six-stage model of moral development, researchers began to question and research if it was possible to move students from a lower stage of moral reasoning to a higher stage. An important pivot point of this stage model was the movement from a stage that focused on self to the next higher stage that recognized the needs of others. This "stage bumping," as Kohlberg (1984) called it, could be facilitated in children and adults. In our goal to promote civility, it is critical to have students begin to recognize the needs of others. Many studies found it was possible to facilitate moral growth in children. A major tool in this effort was the use of questioning skills as a means to get students to delve deeper into the issue. Marvin Berkowitz (1984) studied how individuals *asked questions* to assist students in reflecting and thinking about moral issues. The following represents some strategies in leading a discussion or a seminar with students. Notice how building upon the general knowledge base of the students in the beginning of the lesson combined with the use of the questioning strategies force the student to think, reason, defend, justify, and hopefully be flexible about rethinking her views concerning a piece of writing.

Starting *First, get the facts straight:*

Be sure the content is accurate.
Paraphrase what the issues are.
Make sure all are tuned in.

To start the actual discussions, use open-ended questions:
"What should Person X do? Why, or what are the main reasons?"
Survey the group.

If any of the reasons aren't too clear, then ask clarifying questions. For example:
"Would you say a little more. . . ?"
"Do you mean . . . ?"
"Let me see if I can paraphrase . . . ?"

OR

Ask others in the group if they understand Person X's reasons.

Goal   *Make sure everyone has the chance to make an opening statement. Use "wait time" if needed in questioning.*

Continuing the discussion

Alternative consequences: What might happen if the person did A, B, or C?

Role switch: What would your reasons be if you were Person X, Y, or Z? Put yourself in the shoes of the other person.

Feelings and emotions: How do you suppose Person X is feeling? How might you feel in such a situation? What might be some consequences of those feelings?

Personal experience: Has anything like this ever happened to you? What were your thoughts, feelings, actions? Looking back, is there anything you would change?

Change a key element: "Let's say that the person in the situation is someone you didn't even know, rather than someone very close to you. How might that change things?"

"Some people say": Some say there is never a good reason to break a law. How would you answer that view?

Have discussants talk back and forth to each other: "Henry, how would you answer Amy?" "Jill and Tray seem to be on opposite sides..."

Reaching closure

Issue-related questions: "Now that we viewed it from so many different positions, what are the key elements or most persuasive issues? Is there any particular element that would cause you to switch your view?"

Justice-related questions: "With justice and fairness to all perspectives, what solution would be best?"

(cited in *Educational Psychology: A Developmental Approach,* 4th ed. [1987] by Norman A. Sprinthall and Richard C. Sprinthall, p. 181)

Berkowitz's questioning strategies offer much fodder for those seeking strategies in improving the conversation and ultimately the learning experience for both the leader and student. Although perhaps requiring more involvement on the part of the teacher during the discussion than the Paideia seminar approach, the use of questioning skills is essential in helping children and adults reconsider their ideas relative to the insights of others. Remember, a conversation in its purest sense is designed for all of us, teachers as well as students, to learn from each other. To be successful, an intellectual conversation requires us to listen to the ideas of others and carefully consider our response. We must stifle our impulses to attack or to blurt out agreements and challenges and focus on what is being said, not who is saying it. In other words, we must learn to disagree without becoming disagreeable! Our manners and habits of social civility help us to increase in our intellectual understanding and obligations as civil people. In this way, we improve our macro-civility!

The humanities are replete with opportunities to assist students in developing an intellectual understanding of what it means to be just and civil.

The humanities are replete with opportunities to assist students in developing an intellectual understanding of what it means to be just and civil toward others in our community as well as our nation. As we have learned, simply reading or exposing children to great ideas does not mean they will grasp the significant issues contained within the curriculum. There are developmental as well as pedagogical issues and strategies that we, as educators, must consider. Simply exposing children to great ideas and writing will not have them become great thinkers. However, how we utilize our pedagogical skills just might.

We have briefly examined how the intellect can be developed so that students and those who teach them develop greater insights into the ethical and humane requirements that a civilized person must possess. We will now seek to examine how service learning can be conceived and developed as a tool to promote the civil school.

CHAPTER 7

Service Learning: A Strategy Promoting Civility

by Dr. David Wangaard

The development of a civil culture in school requires the practice of civility. As we have discussed, civility can be developed through the practice of habits that are designed to promote a civil and caring environment. A civil culture also requires education in the moral and intellectual requirements that a civilized person must possess. If we teach the habits and intellectual process for civility we would accomplish much, but we would still be missing an important strategy in promoting civility. To identify this strategy, let us reconsider the definition of civil behavior: "*Civil*—ADJECTIVE: 1. Of, relating to, or befitting a citizen or citizens: civil duties... 7. marked by benevolence."

Civil behavior defines a deeper sense of interrelationships, relationships built on a sense of benefit or benevolence toward others. For example, if we see a person who is upset, should we consider stopping and assisting this person? If we see someone who is physically hurt, do we have a civil responsibility to stop and assist him or her? If we teach civility in our schools, what is our strategy to have students consider their response to those who are less fortunate, economically, socially, or with physical/emotional challenges?

A tremendous school strategy to practice the habits, intellectual requirements, and benevolence of civility is the teaching technique of service learning. Service learning is one way we can engage the students' head, heart, and hand in learning about civility.

Service as Learning

There are easier approaches to practicing the benevolence of civility. We can give money to agencies that seek to help others, such as Habitat for Humanity, faith communities, or the United Way. But fundraising and giving away money does not connect us to the intimate needs of other citizens. It is an indirect form of benevolence and lacks the emotive power of direct service to others. It is fine to raise money for a food kitchen but it is better to work in the food kitchen and have the students reflect on the reasons the food kitchen exists.

The serving of others directly via the giving of our time and energy is a requirement to becoming a civil person.

Our proposition is that the serving of others directly via the giving of our time and energy is a requirement to becoming a civil person. We show our humanity toward others as we serve them. It is our intellect and our habits in action. With this in mind, we believe that schools should play an important role in helping students recognize their obligation to serve others within their school and community. Service learning integrates the teaching method of experiential learning with community service projects. Simply put, it is hands-on learning in service to others. A well-designed service-learning project provides students and teachers opportunities to work together and develop skills and habits of civility. Research supports that service learning has a reciprocal outcome of improving the academic focus and positive learning environment of the classroom as well.

And the Elementary Children Can Lead Us

One of the authors has helped design and implement a service-learning program with the explicit goal of integrating the practice of civility into the program. The program is called Youth: Ethics in Service (YES) and is administered by The School for Ethical Education in Milford, Connecticut. One of the stories from the YES project illustrates how civility can be practiced through the action of service learning.

Fifth graders from a Hockanum Elementary School in East Hartford, Connecticut, served other students in their school in grades K-2, most of whom were identified as autistic or experiencing other special needs. The fifth graders became "buddies" to the students in the special needs class. Once a week, fifth graders left their classes to spend 45 minutes with their buddies. Together they played movement games and completed art projects. The older students helped their buddies build towers, say words and jump on a small trampoline. The fun and games had a purpose. These activities were designed to help the special-education students with their sensory and social development.

To help the fifth graders learn about their roles as teachers, an occupational therapist conducted in-service classes for them. As part of their project, the fifth graders planned and purchased educational materials to assist in their activities with their younger peers. They have used team-building skills acquired through YES to reach a consensus about which items they will purchase and used math skills to figure out what they could afford. Their fifth-grade teacher noted, "It was a great math lesson—real and rewarding."

Each week, the fifth graders reflected on their project experience in a student journal developed by The School for Ethical Education. The students' teacher also noted, "The reflection portion of this program is essential because you need to know how your older buddies are feeling. You want all of the children to leave this experience feeling empowered and good. In addition, reflection activities can also be the perfect opportunity for you as the teacher to offer guidance and make suggestions when they are needed."

The evidence in favor of practicing civility through service learning was noted by the special-education teacher as she observed, "It has been so exciting to watch the looks on the faces of my children as the fifth graders enter my class. They smile and make wonderful eye contact with their older buddies and often initiate the interaction by walking right up to them. These children, who are often reluctant to share themselves, give their fifth-grade friends hugs and share a general level of trust that is miraculous and beautiful. The students in my class know that there are eight older children who recognize their beauty and love them for who they are." She continues, "Other school staff who work along with the buddy students have commented that the students seem to listen and behave better when they are with their buddies."

The biggest challenge to starting the buddy project was finding time when the fifth graders could leave their classrooms. The students were responsible for making up any work they missed and had to maintain good grades in order to stay in the program. Clearly, the special-needs students were benefiting from the buddy program. But what about the older students? Their teacher noted, "The fifth graders have developed a strong sense of leadership, genuine care, love and kindness toward others. They look forward to our sessions as much as the children look forward to their visits. With each meeting, I saw these fifth graders change by leaps and bounds. Their excitement never dwindled, but their confidence soared. Before long, the fifth graders had become little teachers, accomplishing more than many adults could hope to accomplish under similar circumstances. I sometimes wonder whether they realize just how much they have given to their little buddies, and yet I know they recognize all that they have received in return."

> *Students remarked that this project has helped them learn about differences among people and how other people learn. Another young lady added that the buddy program "shows that kids can help people, too."*

The fifth graders were eager to articulate what they like about the program. "I wanted to do this project because I want to be a role model," noted one girl. Other students remarked that this project has helped them learn about differences among people and how other people learn. Another young lady added that the buddy program "shows that kids can help people, too." Stated another, "We have all become a family, but we aren't related."

Clearly, civility was advanced by this project. The benefits of this project are supported by observations made in the literature. Some of these literature references will be shared next. Other lessons from YES will also be shared in this chapter along with a brief review of research that supports service learning, a definition of components to support meaningful service learning and the identification of leadership and social skills that can be practiced during service learning as a means to promote civility.

Assessment of complicated programs like service learning is a challenging process. Determining that a service-learning program is meaningfully implemented requires an intentional focus of evaluation. No one can expect to measure positive outcomes from a program that is not really implemented. In spite of these difficulties, there is a collection of quantitative and qualitative research that supports the value of service learning as a strategy to teach academics and the development of social skills for civility. Students who have participated in meaningful service learning have been noted to demonstrate better school attendance, personal and social responsibility, communication skills, and work orientation than those who were not engaged in service learning (Corporation for National Service, 1997; The Search Institute, 2000). In some cases, studies revealed that student academic work improves for students involved in service learning (Leming, 1999), and there is often a positive correlation observed between successful service learning and the engagement of service in later years (Melchior & Orr, 1995). In addition, researchers have observed that participants in service learning express a higher sense of social connection and an appreciation for shared community values or character goals that support civility (Skinner & Chapman, 1999).

These research-based observations are all excellent outcomes of service learning. Certainly in our struggle to create civil classrooms and schools, we can use a teaching strategy with all the positive attributes associated with meaningful service learning. Meaningful service learning is the key to unlock the benefits of the strategy. Let us look at what defines a meaningful service-learning program.

Meaningful Service Learning

Service learning has evolved in the past 20 years and developed national support groups that include the Corporation for National and Community Service and the National Youth Leadership Council. These two groups have helped to create a body of definitions and research to support service learning. While service learning is still a maturing field of practice, it is generally agreed that the following seven components should exist for a meaningful service-learning program:

1. Students will be given age-appropriate responsibility to help in the leadership, planning and implementation of the service project.
2. Project work will include time for training and preparation of youth and adult participants and includes the establishment of clear project objectives.
3. The project will be meaningful and meet a real need in the community. The community may be defined inside or outside of the service organization (school).
4. Relevant academic content is integrated into the project with the development of specific content rubrics to define successful mastery of academic goals.
5. Participants build social connections within the project team and with the community being served.
6. Reflection is practiced during and after project completion to aid in personal and project development.
7. There is a summative evaluation process that assesses the achievement of project objectives.

Each component to support a meaningful service-learning project is worthy of its own book chapter. As this is a text on civility, we refer the reader to page 117 as a brainstorming and evaluation rubric to promote meaningful service learning. Our attention will focus on aspects of selected components and how student leadership and explicit team roles (component 1) can help establish clear project objectives and expectations for civility (component 2) while building social connections through a process of consensus-based decision making (component 5) and practicing individual and team reflection (component 6).

Student Leadership: Team Roles

Assigning team roles is a useful strategy to increase student engagement with learning and to promote individual contributions to their team (Johnson, Johnson & Holubec, 1994). Kagan (1994) notes the importance of developing positive interdependence through the assignment of roles for the success of the team. Each student becomes responsible to his team for the completion of a specific role. Roles are flexible and can be identified in a variety of ways. A selection of useful roles is identified here as examples of responsibilities that students can perform to implement a meaningful service project while promoting civility during the process.

Roles are most useful in small teams (four to six students) where each student can be assigned specific responsibilities during the life of a service project. Some typical team roles and their definitions include: *Leader*—organizes and helps pick roles, checks understanding of assignments, checks completion of assigned tasks; *Time Keeper*—keeps track of available time for task, helps focus discussion and activities; *Recorder*—keeps notes on team ideas, summarizes team products, organizes products to publish team results; *Balancer*—tracks participation of team members, encourages input of all members; *Reporter/PR*—monitors the team's participation and the team's impact on others, provides oral reports for team; *Reflector*—tracks the work process used by the team, helps team reflect on process and goals, asks the question, "Are we working well together?"

Assignment of defined roles helps create the positive interdependence for a team to flourish during service learning. Students recognize their accountability to the team to complete a task and students focusing on their roles help a team avoid conflicts in missed or overlapping assignments.

Teachers need to teach and help the students practice their role for these leadership assignments to be meaningful. Experienced teachers recognize the need to begin role assignments with an awareness of how student temperament may influence their success in the role. Creating outcomes for each role will also help form the basis for the evaluation of team participation. This highlights the need for the teacher to work in collaboration with the team in order to identify the responsibilities of each team member and their team role. Team roles thus give students a framework to practice civil cooperation in the implementation of a service project while providing the teacher an additional rubric to evaluate student participation.

In our field experience with YES, we have recognized that students take on a greater sense of responsibility for their projects when they volunteer or are assigned team roles. These roles, however, may also create tension in a team when students with dominating personalities control all the leadership functions. Teachers are wise to provide opportunities for roles to be evaluated and changed during the course of the project.

Roles are most useful in small teams where each student can be assigned specific responsibilities.

Clear Objectives and Social Connections

As discussed in previous chapters, students and adults must have a sense of belonging or membership in a class to experience a desire to demonstrate civility. The students' sense of membership in a community, a class or a team can be cultivated by a proactive teacher. Many authors have noted the value of developing a sense of team or community to achieve the academic and social goals in schools (Boyte & Farr, 1996; Developmental Studies Center, 1995). In the YES program, many students noted every year how pleased they were to be part of a team that made a positive contribution to their community. Research by the Developmental Studies Center (1995) has noted, "As human beings, one of our most powerful and basic needs is to form affective bonds with others. Belonging to a group provides emotional support and security, and the purposes and activities of the groups that we belong to are an important source of meaning in our lives." One strategy to build social connection is the explicit identification and practice of shared objectives and norms that support positive school environments and reduce student engagement in uncivil behavior (Charney, 1991; Clayton, Ballif-Spanvill & Hunsaker, 2001).

"As human beings, one of our most powerful and basic needs is to form affective bonds with others."

A positive sense of community can be greatly assisted by engaging the participants in the leadership and establishment of behavioral norms and values for the team. We use the word team to represent any class, club, extracurricular team, or service-learning team. Students from kindergarten to 12th grade can become engaged in an age-appropriate process to identify values or character goals that will define behaviors or the civil norms for their work together. A service-learning project is not required to establish these goals; however, a service-learning project provides many opportunities to practice character traits to complete a successful project. As facilitated by a teacher or student leader, students could work cooperatively to complete the following worksheet and identify and define the character goals for their project.

Defining Our Team Expectations

Work individually and from the following list of character traits (or other traits you identify). Select two or three character traits that could guide the expectations of your team.

> **Caring, Cooperation, Citizenship, Fairness, Honesty, Integrity, Loyalty, Optimism, Perseverance, Pursuit of Excellence, Respect for Authority, Respect for Others, Respect for Property, Responsibility, Trustworthiness**

Character Goal: _____

Character Goal: _____

Character Goal: _____

As a team, have a student leader facilitate a discussion to list and tally all student responses. For example, 10 students selected respect as a trait to guide your team's expectations—Respect: 10, and eight students selected cooperation—Cooperation: 8. After all responses are tallied and reported, identify the top three character traits selected by your team. Record your top three team character goals in the blanks below and write specific descriptions of what each character trait would look like if it were demonstrated (students and adults) during the service-learning project.

Character Goal:_____ is demonstrated when

_____

_____

_____

Character Goal:_____ is demonstrated when

_____

_____

_____

Character Goal:_____ is demonstrated when

_____

_____

_____

As a team, discuss and edit your team's character expectations and create a poster to remind the team of this exercise and your shared expectations.

Two things are accomplished by completing the Defining our Team Expectations worksheet. Students are united in their shared identification of a vocabulary for character goals and their character goals are defined with specific behavioral outcomes that support civility. Identifying and defining the character goals for the conduct of any project helps build a positive expectation for the team and creates a foundation for civil cooperation. A second strategy to maintain civility and social connections on teams is the use of consensus-based decision making. Cero-a-Cinco is one specific strategy to support the goal of consensus building.

Consensus Building: Cero-a-Cinco

Consensus can be defined as a general agreement for action by a team. Consensus does not necessarily mean unanimous agreement, although a super majority of students (65%+) and the teacher should form the core of agreement for consensus. The strategy of consensus building brings attention to the ideas and opinions of those holding a minority opinion within the team. While unanimous agreement is not necessary, consensus-based decision-making helps to avoid the creation of team resistors. Resistors can be created when the minority opinion is ignored and perceived to be disrespected. Students can be taught how to arrive at team consensus through the use of Cero-a-Cinco.

In the YES program, Cero-a-Cinco has been shown to provide a method for everyone on a team to express their support or concern for an idea or proposal. Skillful student team leaders can use the Cero-a-Cinco strategy to improve ideas or proposals and achieve a super majority of group support.

The Cero-a-Cinco consensus-building strategy can begin whenever a team has an idea or proposal that requires a group decision. After a proposal is made, the team leader should seek discussion and clarification of the proposal prior to requesting that all team members vote by showing cinco (five) fingers down to cero (zero) fingers. It is important for the team leader to facilitate everyone's display of fingers at the same time. Students should be encouraged to display and not change their finger ballot during the voting. This procedure helps avoid peer pressure altering students' true opinions. Team members rank their support of a proposal with their fingers applying the ranking scale in Table 1.

Table 1. Cero-A-Cinco consensus building ranking scale.

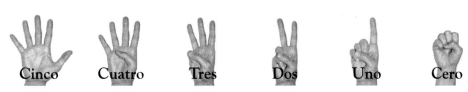

Cinco   Cuatro   Tres   Dos   Uno   Cero

Cinco (five) fingers defines strong support for the idea.

Cuatro (four) fingers indicates good support and maybe a suggestion for improvement.

Tres (three) fingers notes team member support, but there may be some concerns.

Dos (two) fingers informs the leader that a team member will support the proposal, but would like to seek some modifications of the idea.

Uno (one finger) notes a team member will go along for consensus, however; he/she has concerns about the proposal that could be changed.

Cero (zero) fingers informs the leader of resistance to the proposal and that this team member does not think this idea is viable and does not want to support it.

During the display of finger ballots, the team leader should note the range of responses for the proposal and, if there is not an obvious consensus, seek feedback to improve the idea from those who displayed one, two, or three fingers. If multiple ballots are anticipated, the team recorder should note the total number of fingers displayed. This information can help document changes in team support for modified or new proposals. During all balloting and discussion of suggestions, the team leader and team reflector should help the team remain consistent with the character goals identified earlier to promote civil dialogue.

The process of cero-a-cinco can move a team quickly through proposal, balloting, discussion, and balloting new or modified proposals. If a super majority is not achieved in the first ballot of cero-a-cinco, a wise team leader will solicit the feedback of individuals who display less support. Respectfully listening to concerns of team members and team consideration of modified proposals can help create better project ideas and maintain a strong consensus for team progress.

Cero-a-cinco is a useful strategy to promote civil discourse and negotiation within a team and help avoid the resentments and resistance that can build in teams that use only majority approval for decision-making.

Reflection is a final skill to be presented here to advance civility in schools and for service-learning teams. Reflection strategies will be presented that can help individuals or groups maintain their focus on positive character and the demonstration of civility.

Reflection for Learning and Civility

Someone once noted, "I do not learn from my experience, but I do learn by reflecting about my experience." Reflection can be a powerful tool to promote learning and civility. For our purpose, reflection will be defined as thinking about your past, present, or future experiences in light of previously stated character goals and the Golden Rule. Teachers can help students select topics for reflection, a medium to practice reflection (writing, discussion, art, drama), and the scope of reflection (narrow, broad, self or others). We will discuss how varying the scope of reflection can help reflection activities remain fresh and relevant to advance service learning and civility.

Given the time pressures that students and teachers face in schools, reflection is often overlooked or relegated to a short oral debriefing session at the end of a service-learning project. The planned integration of various forms of reflection during and at the close of projects does require additional time and effort. We argue that the time and effort used to reflect individually and as a team will provide increased mastery for team goals (academic, athletic, or project) and reinforce the practice of civility.

To keep reflection activities engaging, teachers and student reflectors should consider how they might vary the medium of reflection. Team or small-group discussions and journaling are tried and true media for reflection. Creative leaders can add the mediums of various forms of art, drama, poetry and/or group games that catalyze specific discussion questions. A Bridgeport, Connecticut,

> *"I do not learn from my experience, but I do learn by reflecting about my experience."*

high-school team in the YES program used their reflection time to encourage the writing of reflective poems. Some of these poems became lyrics to songs and ultimately the recording of a music and poetry CD. The students used the proceeds from the sale of this CD to continue the support of a homeless shelter they were assisting during their service-learning project.

The scope of reflection can also vary and we suggest three variations that include: wide-angle, microscope, or mirror reflection and can be applied to any medium of reflection. Wide-angle reflection is described by having participants think about the big picture of their experience. For example, if students were engaged in a mentoring project, a wide-angle reflection topic might seek to have the participants consider reflecting on the range of reasons mentees might need a mentor and the various benefits mentees might experience from their involvement with a mentoring program. As a second variation, microscope reflection can request participants to look at some detail of their project experience. Using the previous example of  mentoring, a microscope reflection goal could be to have students consider one element of their project work. For example, mentors could be given an opportunity to reflect on their last meeting with a mentee and asked to describe helpful communication skills practiced during the meeting. A third reflection technique seeks participants to look in a mirror and reflect on their own actions, experiences, and beliefs that relate to a project. Mentors could be requested to provide a mirror reflection that describes their own self-evaluation during the mentoring project. Mentors could be asked, "How does their personal participation help the team reach its overall project goals?" These reflection strategies can lead to useful discussion sessions to support the development of moral reasoning as discussed in Chapter Six.

Wide-angle, microscope, and mirror reflection provide teachers different focus points to promote relevant reflection during and after team projects. Varying the scope of reflection and mediums of reflection can help keep reflection activities fresh and engaging for students. Effective reflection helps teams maintain an active memory of stated team character goals as well helping to review and then guide project work. Several reflection questions are provided on page 120 as examples of possible topics for students in service-learning projects.

The goal of creating civil classrooms and schools requires the practice of behaviors that can help all students succeed academically and socially while developing leadership skills to reach project goals. Service learning and the practice of setting character goals, using team roles, cero-a-cinco and regular reflection is a dynamic set of skills and strategies to support student success and the demonstration of civility in schools.

Evaluation Rubric for Service-Learning Teams

Team/School:_____

Teacher/Facilitator: _____

	Weak	Needs Work	Strong
Student Participation			
Students are involved in selecting S-L projects.			
Students are involved in developing S-L projects.			
Students are involved in implementing S-L projects.			
Students are involved in assessing S-L projects.			
S-L initiatives are available for all students who are interested.			
Students complete a minimum of 30 hours of service over the course of project(s).			
Training/Preparation			
Program includes training, supervision, and monitoring of SL and all youth and adults involved.			
Students and adults recognize strategic planning steps.			
Project has clear objectives established to define successful conclusion.			
Students are monitored during service activities.			
Service recipients have time to meet with students before service.			
The community being served has input into the project.			
Teachers are trained in components of meaningful SL.			
Students are trained in cooperative work skills (team building, team roles, consensus decision making).			
Meaningful Projects			
S-L students are engaged in responsible and challenging actions for the common good that meet genuine needs in the school or community.			
Needs assessment activities (research, talking with community members, issue analysis) are done before beginning any S-L activity.			

	Weak	Needs Work	Strong
Academic/Curricular connections			
S-L activities are directly tied to regular class objectives and activities.			
Portions of S-L activities occur during regular school hours.			
Students identify or are aware of the learning goals at the outset of a S-L project.			
Team and Community Building			
Students use cooperative work strategies.			
Project team identifies shared values to be demonstrated during project.			
Students identify and use team roles to share project responsibilities.			
Students use consensus-building strategies.			
Students learn about the people, places, or things being served.			
Students can tell one story about the people, places, or things served.			
Reflection			
Preparation (pre-reflection) time is given to students and adults before service.			
Structured student reflection encourages critical thinking and is central to fulfillment of curricular objectives.			
Reflection is done through a variety of media (written, spoken, arts).			
Students recognize and practice different "lens" of reflection—microscope, wide-angle, mirror.			
Reflection activities are completed regularly during the project (for example, 2-3x/month).			
Students engaged in reflection activities designed to stimulate discussion of shared values and the principles behind the Golden Rule.			

	Weak	Needs Work	Strong
Evaluation			
A formal evaluation is completed that assesses project meeting stated objectives.			
The community served provides feedback on the value and effectiveness of service.			
All members of S-L project have opportunity to provide input into evaluation.			

Number of Students: _____   Number of Adults: _____

Number of Service & Reflection & Planning Hours: _____ (X number of students)

Type of Project: ☐ Human Needs   ☐ Safety   ☐ Environment   ☐ Education

Suggested Reflection Topics

Topic Domain	Reflection Topic
Wide Angle	Brainstorm all the possible strategies your team might use to address the community need your service project will address.
Wide Angle	Identify as many resources (people, talents, money, tools) that your team has available to support your team in reaching its project goals.
Wide Angle	What do you see your team learning through this project experience? Work with your teacher to link your possible learning objectives to subjects you are studying in school.
Microscope	Contrast how students can help address a community need as compared with local experts.
Microscope	Why is the Golden Rule important in guiding our choices of behavior?
Microscope	How is your team demonstrating the character goals you established at the start of the project?
Mirror	Describe why your service-learning project is important to you.
Mirror	Without words, sketch an aspect of your project that you really enjoy.
Mirror	With one to two word descriptors, list all the things (academically, socially, skill development, about your community, about you) that you learned during this service project.

CHAPTER 8

Some Specific Strategies to Promote Civility

Perhaps now you're ready to begin the process of enhancing the civility in your school. Where might you begin? First, you must remember that there are three areas you wish to involve in creating the civil school: manners or practices that promote civility; literature, narratives and the remainder of the curriculum, which are used to enhance discussions on civility; and the opportunity to serve each other. Start by asking, "What positive social habits and intellectual preciosities should a child have when he/she leaves your school?" Take a moment and think on this. Once this is established, the hard part begins. What practices must the school family implement to make these ideals a reality?

We have selected some small strategies that might facilitate your efforts in developing or improving the civil climate of your school. Hopefully, this will act as a catalyst as you begin your dialogue with your peers, students, parents, and others in the community.

Be the moral compass.

All adults must strive to live a life that is a walking advertisement for civility and the way we want our children to treat others. We can develop a list of strategies and practices that will remind children of the importance of civility. We can work to develop good habits of kindness and politeness. These are important. But our children will pay more attention to what we do than what we say. We as the adults in the school should strive to become a "sermon in shoes" for our children. Every day we should look in the mirror and pledge to live a life of civility for ourselves and for our children. We will not be perfect in our efforts but if we know and commit to our objectives we have a better chance of achieving them.

Reminders.

Students need reminders of what is important in the classroom as well as throughout the school. For example, a coach may have a reminder of the importance of sportsmanship posted in the locker room. This reminder is further reinforced via her lessons and model- ing of sportsmanship for her athletes. Perhaps another teacher posts reminders of how others are to be treated within the confines of the classroom. As previously noted in Chapter One, a discussion about the Golden Rule reminds students and adults of their obligation toward others. Note, it is not enough simply to post The Golden Rule: A Global View poster (2003, Character Development Group), one must also take the time to discuss the meaning of these maxims. How is the Golden Rule applied in your classroom? Your life? One can also post maxims that promote reflection on civility throughout a classroom or school. Following are some maxims that could merit discussion on the importance of civility:

Life is not so short, but that there is always time enough for courtesy.
  —Ralph Waldo Emerson: Letters and Social Aims

Good manners are the technique of expressing consideration for the feelings of others.
  —Alice Duer Miller

If a man be gracious and courteous to strangers, it shows he is a citizen of the world, and that his heart is no island cut off from other lands but a continent that joins to them.
  —Francis Bacon: Of Goodness and Goodness of Nature

Civility costs nothing and buys everything.
  —Lady Mary Wortley Montague: letter in 1756

It is incredible what a difference it makes to one's feelings towards
the whole human race when one is treated with politeness and kindness in buses,
trains, trams, subways, ferries, stores, ships and streets.
—*John Cowper Powys: The Meaning of Culture*

Politeness, that cementer of friendships and soother of enmities...
—*Marguerite Blessington: The Repealers*

Friendship cannot live with Ceremony, nor without Civility.
—*Benjamin Franklin: Poor Richard's Almanack*

Punctuality is the politeness of kings.
—*Louis XVIII*

Politeness has been well defined as benevolence in small things.
—*Macaulay: Essays*

Be civil to all: sociable to many; familiar with few; friend to one: enemy to none.
—*Benjamin Franklin: Poor Richard's Almanack*

Everyone who receives the protection of society owes a return for the benefit.
—*John Stuart Mill: On Liberty*

There is little pleasure in the world that is sincere and true beside that
of doing our duty and doing good; no other is comparable to this.
—*John Tillotson, Archbishop of Canterbury*

I slept and dreamed that life was pleasure; I woke and saw that life was service;
I served and discovered that service was pleasure.
—*Rabindranath Tagore*

Service is the rent you pay for room on this earth.
—*Shirley Chisholm*

Some people strengthen society just by being the kind of people they are.
—*John W. Gardner: No Easy Victories*

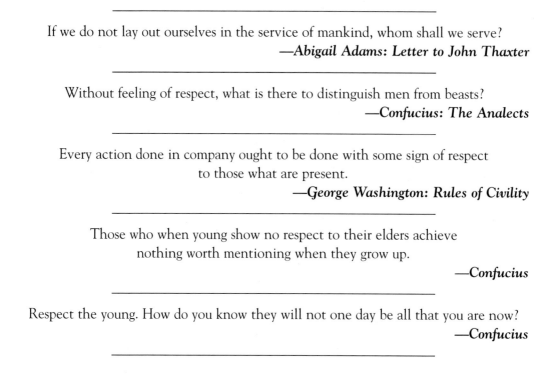

If we do not lay out ourselves in the service of mankind, whom shall we serve?

—*Abigail Adams: Letter to John Thaxter*

Without feeling of respect, what is there to distinguish men from beasts?

—*Confucius: The Analects*

Every action done in company ought to be done with some sign of respect to those what are present.

—*George Washington: Rules of Civility*

Those who when young show no respect to their elders achieve nothing worth mentioning when they grow up.

—*Confucius*

Respect the young. How do you know they will not one day be all that you are now?

—*Confucius*

Teachers in the hall.

Part of teaching civility is modeling it. If we want students to be kind to each other, we must be kind to them. One way of doing this is to greet students in the hall. This is not a formal greeting but rather a time to dialogue with students. The authors have found that if faculty members stand in their doorways and have conversations with students during class change, there is less disorder in the hall. We do not believe this is because we are catching the students before they do something bad; rather we feel it is because teachers by their doorways in conversation with children exhibit civility and caring toward students who desire positive interactions with adults. Just commit as a faculty to stand in your doorway as much as possible and interact with the students. You will be surprised at how this simple act promotes civility toward others.

Celebrate examples of civility toward others.

It never hurts to recognize an act of kindness or caring from one person to another. Recognition can be through an assembly focused on recognizing examples of caring and kindness within the school. Perhaps the educators or the students nominate the recipients. Their parents are asked to attend if possible and certificates are handed out. These students are celebrated as leaders within the school. Another way to recognize acts of civility and kindness is for the teacher to go quietly to the student's desk and to thank the child individually with perhaps a hand on the shoulder of the child. We believe children value one-on-one time with significant adults in their lives. This quiet recognition further cements this bond. Another way to further this recognition is to mail a letter home to a parent describing what the child did or continues to do to promote civility and kindness within the classroom. If you visit the home of the child, you may see these letters on a refrigerator. If not there, you can at least hope they are posted in the heart of the parent. High school students can also receive commendations or recognition that can be placed in their permanent records or college or work recommendations.

Developing a mission statement on civility.

The mission statement of the United States Military Academy is:

> **To educate, train, and inspire** the Corps of Cadets so that each graduate is a commissioned leader of character committed to the values of Duty, Honor, Country: professional growth throughout a career as an officer in the United States Army: and a lifetime of selfless service to the nation.

Each school should develop a mission statement that focuses on the importance of civility in their actions toward others. This should apply to the students as well as the adults in the building. This is essential so that everyone will know where the school is headed. Remember, if you do not know where you are going, any road will take you there. A mission statement that addresses the importance of civility in the learning environment is a reminder of the importance of civility in the life of the school.

Develop a pledge of civility.

The mission statement provides an overview of the values of a school. A pledge of civility is a quick reminder to students and teachers of what is important. In the mission statement, we featured the mission statement of the United States Military Academy. Let us now consider the pledge from the Cadet Honor Code: "A cadet shall not lie, cheat, steal, or tolerate those who do."

Isn't that simple? Yet it is to the point and clearly states the obligation of the cadet. If we practiced this pledge would we not enhance our character and promote greater civility in our lives and within our schools? A pledge of civility exists to issue a standard by which we as adults and the children in our care might live. Schools as well as classrooms can develop their own pledge of civility. The pledge should be kept simple so that children and adults can memorize it. It should also state how we should try and live our lives.

The use of a personal greeting.

We have learned this practice from Charlie Abourjilie: greet your children with a handshake in the morning or at the beginning of each class for those who do not have the same children for the

A personal greeting is "the transfer of positive energy at the door!"

entire day. Dr. Hal Urban refers to this as "the transfer of positive energy at the door!" We just feel it is a wonderful way to start a morning or a class. It also helps children learn a professional way of greeting someone. For those who may shy away from handshakes or desire to use other forms of greetings, we recommend a pat on the back or a "high five." Above all, try to call the child by his first or called name. Some in high school greet students with a "Mr." or a "Ms." What is important is a personal greeting.

Cafeteria recognition of civility.

Some cafeteria staff in Chattanooga, Tennessee, work with the rest of the school to promote civility. Specifically, staff and teachers work with students on developing good manners while eating in the cafeteria. They take the time to recognize students and classes that are cleaning-up after their meals and practicing good manners while at the table. Some cafeterias have reminders of the requirements of good manners on bulletin boards as one enters the serving line. The reasoning is quite simple, how children come into and leave the cafeteria is how they will return to their next class. This allows the cafeteria to send a message that manners and civility matter in the cafeteria as well as throughout the school. Another good practice for cafeteria workers is to take the time to learn the names of the children and seek to speak to as many as possible. We should also expect our children in the cafeteria to be polite to the workers as well as the workers being polite to the children. Remember, "May I help you?" sounds much better than, "What do you want?"

My job as an educator is not to like all the children I teach. It is to try to love them.

Student government as civil facilitators.

We believe that student government can play a role in promoting civility in the life of a school. One school's student government decided to tackle the issue of cursing in the hallways and in other public areas. They decided that they would put the word cursing in the familiar red circle with the line through the word cursing. These were posted throughout the school. In addition, they asked teachers to stand outside their doors if possible and talk to "guilty" students about their choice of words! The principal reported that there was a tremendous reduction in the use of inappropriate language in the school. Students can be part of the solution to the problems that plague us. Sometimes all we need to do is ask or seek their input.

Consider that you may not always like all the children you teach, but try to love them.

If we love our children we will expect and model civility toward them. Consider your own life. We imagine that you have friends that you may not approve of all that they do. They are still your friends and you like them. But, when you love someone you want only the best for him. You want him to reach the highest levels of achievement and civility. Love is far greater than liking someone. Loving demands standards that liking fails to demand or even ask. As a parent we know this is true. There are days you may not like your child, but you will never fail to love that child. We should try to achieve the same attitude toward our students.

Recognize those that are contributing to the school and community by their service efforts.

Many high schools have an academic hall of fame that highlights students who have achieved outstanding academic and performance goals. Most likely, they have a trophy case that highlights their athletic efforts. Consider having a Service/Caring Hall of Fame. Within this, highlight students who are serving others in the school and community. Call local faith communities as well as social organizations. Ask them to send the names or pictures of students who are contributing to your community through their organizations. One principal sent letters to community organizations and requested that they notify him when students were in service to others, through their organizations. He sought to make personal contact with these students as well as thanking them over the intercom on every Monday.

Post service opportunities in your school and in the community.

Student and/or teacher organizations could seek to establish a service board for the school. The board would list groups or individuals that are seeking assistance within the school or community. The school could post listings for tutors or for students to assist those with special needs within the school or other neighboring schools. Groups engaging in building Habitat for Humanity houses could send flyers to schools and notify students of house raising opportunities. Social and faith groups should also be encouraged to send their notices. If possible, we should try and recognize students via newsletters or morning announcements that are contributing to the improvement of our school and community.

Take time to talk with the students about civility.

This will include the importance of civil practices and the civility that comes from caring about others, as well as the intellectual awareness on the importance of civility that we garner through the humanities and sciences. Have students keep a reflection journal. Ask to read and comment in it. We need to touch the students' minds as well as their hearts.

Develop, post, and occasionally review a teacher civility pledge.

This pledge should focus on how we, the teachers, should treat our students during the class time we spend together. In her book, *Growing Character: 99 Successful Strategies for the Elementary Classroom* (2003), Deb Brown illustrates one of her teacher pledges that she develops and posts each year. Her 2002-2003 pledge is listed below:

RESPECT   I will listen to my students.
I will speak in a soft and respectful voice.

FAIRNESS   I will treat each student fairly, without prejudice.
I will be available to answer student questions.

CITIZENSHIP   I will be a good role model for kids.
I will make contributions for the good of our school.

During staff meetings, have teachers share how they are utilizing the curriculum to promote civility.

If you are teaching in the elementary school, divide this by grade level. In the middle school, utilize your teams and in the high school, divide this via the disciplines. For example, a fifth grade team in an elementary school could describe how they have teamed fifth graders to work with first graders to improve their cafeteria manners. A middle-school team could describe how they developed a student/teacher team that meets to address issues of kindness, or lack of, within their team. A high school physical education department could describe how they are incorporating sportsmanship in all their games and activities.

Develop a thank-you tree.

While working with schools in Florida, one of the authors discovered a "thank-you" tree located in the office area of an elementary school. The adults in the school place thank-you leaves for others in the school who, through their going beyond the call of duty, have improved the civil life of the school. The thank-you leaves may feature teachers thanking cafeteria workers or custodians for going beyond what is required to help make their school a better place. It may include teachers thanking teachers or teacher assistants as well as a custodian thanking an office worker. The people of that school simply take the time to thank others for contributing to the civility within the school. As a way of celebration, once a month the entire staff assembles for cake, ice cream and a passing out of the thank-you leaves from the tree. It is a wonderful time for celebrating and remembering that everyone in a school matters.

Recognize civility on the report card.

Have a place on a report card where the adults in a school can add some comments to the child as well as the parents on the acts of civility the child exhibits in the school. Remember, all parents appreciate it when their children are complimented based on their character.

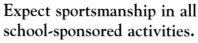

Expect sportsmanship in all school-sponsored activities.

Not everyone will achieve greatness in athletics, yet all students can develop the habits of good sportsmanship, both during and after an athletic competition. Remember, this must start with the coaches, who must act as the moral compass. Through the coaches' modeling and teaching, the importance of sportsmanship is received and practiced by the players. Guilford County Schools in North Carolina recently recognized the high schools that had no suspensions from any of their teams based on inappropriate student and/or coach activities during the previous sports year. This recognition was about how they played the games, not whether they won or lost. Good sportsmanship counts.

Ask for insights from parents on what they are doing in the home to promote civility.

Many parents are working extremely hard on building civility within their homes. Perhaps they have developed some strategies that could prove beneficial for other parents. Have parents send in to the guidance counselor their tips on promoting civility in the home. These tips can then be incorporated in the school newsletter with descriptions of what the school is doing to reinforce and, if needed, model, teach, and demand civility from their students.

Seek examples of civility toward others from the media and use the school newspaper to celebrate individuals or groups that are promoting civility.

Most newspapers, as well as local television news, will regularly feature individuals or groups within the community who have worked to contribute to the welfare of others. Either newspaper articles or clips from the news are good conversation starters to share with students during the class day or during morning meetings, homeroom, or advisor/advisee time. Another way to encourage students to seek out these sources is to have them take responsibility for surfing the Internet or local media outlets for stories on individuals who have worked for the betterment of others. Still another extension would be to have the school newspaper focus on individuals or groups in the school that are working to promote a more civil and caring climate. There could also be featured stories on these individuals or groups with the name of contact persons for those who desire to get involved.

Have faculty discussions on readings involving civility.

We have advocated the use of seminars or conversations on the humanities for students. Why not include this for the adults in the school? School personnel should continue their intellectual development. What better way than to have regularly scheduled seminars or conversations, before or after school, involving great ideas. What adult would not gain from reading or rereading King's "Letter From a Birmingham Jail"? What about excerpts from Plato's *Republic* or *The Crito*? What about revisiting the Declaration of Independence or the Bill of Rights? How about *Hamlet*? Believe me, Shakespeare has gotten much more insightful as you have aged. A school could seek out readings from other parts of the world. We could compare and contrast notions of civility and obligations within various cultures. This may help us under-

> *What adult would not gain from reading or rereading King's "Letter From a Birmingham Jail"?*

stand the perspectives that children from throughout the world bring to our classrooms. Equally important to what we garner from the conversations is the practice of sitting down and listening respectfully to the thoughts of our peers. How can we expect our students to do this if we are reluctant to offer the same courtesy to others?

Tools for Planning and Implementing Expectations and Practices to Promote Civility

In a previous book, *Rules and Procedures for Character Education: The First Step Toward School Civility* (1999), Dr. Vincent established forms that would help an entire school community begin to examine its expectations and practices needed to promote core practices in developing habits of civility for everyone in the school. The forms are sequential in nature, with each form building on the previous one. For example, the first form asks that individuals state their expectations for building a civil school. Other forms guide individuals as they combine into small groups to reach a consensus before seeking total school consensus.

Many schools reported that these forms helped them focus their efforts in developing a more civil school. Others have reported that after doing the exercise with their faculty, they involved their students in the same process. Most reported a great deal of consensus between the faculty and students. Still others have used them only within their classrooms to establish buy-in and support from their students. We have updated and are including these forms within the present work. Please feel free to work through the forms as an individual teacher, a team of teachers or an entire school staff as you seek to develop consistent expectations and practices throughout your class or school environment. And remember, we must model what we expect from our students.

FORM 1—EXPECTATIONS

Individual Work Page for Expectations

Brainstorm a list of expectations that you personally desire of your students. At this point, just get your ideas down. You will combine and omit some in the next step.

Develop two to four expectations that will guide your efforts to promote civility in your school. For example:

1. Students and adults in this school are respectful of each other.

_____

_____

2. _____

_____

_____

3. _____

_____

_____

4. _____

_____

_____

FORM 2—EXPECTATIONS

Small Group's List of Expectations to Promote Civility

Share your expectations to promote civility with the small group of four to six educators. Each person's expectations will be written down below. Do not duplicate the expectations. Just put a check mark beside duplicate ones. You may need additional space.

List your expectations from the small group.

_____

_____

_____

_____

_____

_____

_____

_____

_____

_____

_____

_____

_____

_____

_____

_____

_____

FORM 3—EXPECTATIONS

Small Group's Consensus on Expectations

Examine the small group's list of expectations from Form 2. Combine and delete until you can reach consensus on two to four expectations. These will be shared with the total group.

Group Consensus

List your two to four expectations that the small group concurs upon.

1. _____

   _____

   _____

2. _____

   _____

   _____

3. _____

   _____

   _____

4. _____

   _____

   _____

FORM 4—EXPECTATIONS

Total Group's Listing of the Expectations

List the expectations from Form 3 of each of the small groups. Do not duplicate the expectations. Just put a check mark beside duplicate ones. You may need additional space.

Group Consensus

List the small group expectations from each group to create a total school listing of expectations.

_____

_____

_____

_____

_____

_____

_____

_____

_____

_____

_____

_____

_____

Now see if you can reach consensus as a group on two to four expectations that will guide your efforts in developing practices to promote civility in your school. If you are not able to do this as an entire faculty, form a team to take the recommendations from Form 4. This team will seek to develop consensus on the expectations and report its findings to the entire faculty. Afterward, you can begin your work on the practices that will be modeled and developed for everyone in the school.

FORM 5—PRACTICES BASED ON EXPECTATIONS

Individual Work Page on Practices

Taking the total group's two to four expectations, write two to four practices under each expectation. This will be shared with the small group. For example:

EXPECTATION #1

Students and adults in this school are respectful of each other.

Practices

1. Students and adults in this school use polite words such as: "please," "thank you," "excuse me," "may I."

   _____

   _____

2. _____

   _____

   _____

3. _____

   _____

   _____

4. _____

   _____

   _____

EXPECTATION 2 *(FORM 5: Individual Work Page on Practices)*

Practices

1. _____

_____

_____

2. _____

_____

_____

3. _____

_____

_____

4. _____

_____

_____

EXPECTATION 3 *(FORM 5: Individual Work Page on Practices)*

Practices

1. _____

_____

_____

2. _____

_____

_____

3. _____

_____

_____

4. _____

_____

_____

EXPECTATION 4 *(FORM 5: Individual Work Page on Practices)*

Practices

1. _____

_____

_____

2. _____

_____

_____

3. _____

_____

_____

4. _____

_____

_____

FORM 6—PRACTICES

Small Group's Work Page on Practices

List the total group's two to four expectations and practices below. As a group, write practices under each expectation, with each member sharing his or her ideas. Don't duplicate the practices. If it has been said, just put a check beside it to denote agreement.

EXPECTATION 1 (FORM 6: Small Group's Work Page on Practices)

_____

Practices

_____

_____

_____

_____

_____

_____

_____

_____

_____

_____

_____

_____

_____

_____

EXPECTATION 2 *(FORM 6: Small Group's Work Page on Practices)*

Practices

EXPECTATION 3 (FORM 6: *Small Group's Work Page on Practices*)

Practices

EXPECTATION 4 *(FORM 6: Small Group's Work Page on Practices)*

Practices

1. _____

_____

_____

2. _____

_____

_____

3. _____

_____

_____

4. _____

_____

_____

FORM 7—PRACTICES

Small Group's Consensus on Practices

Take the entire list of practices agreed to on Form 6, and as an entire group, develop two to four practices under each expectation. This will be the final work of the small group.

EXPECTATION 1 (FORM 7: Small Group's Consensus on Practices)

_____

Practices

1. _____

   _____

   _____

2. _____

   _____

   _____

3. _____

   _____

   _____

4. _____

   _____

   _____

EXPECTATION 2 *(FORM 7: Small Group's Consensus on Practices)*

_____

Practices

1. _____

_____

_____

2. _____

_____

_____

3. _____

_____

_____

4. _____

_____

_____

EXPECTATION 3 *(FORM 7: Small Group's Consensus on Practices)*

Practices

1. _____

_____

_____

2. _____

_____

_____

3. _____

_____

_____

4. _____

_____

_____

EXPECTATION 4 *(FORM 7: Small Group's Consensus on Practices)*

_____

Practices

1. _____

   _____

   _____

2. _____

   _____

   _____

3. _____

   _____

   _____

4. _____

   _____

   _____

FORM 8—PRACTICES

Practices from Small Group to Total Group

Because the small group reached consensus on the practices on Form 7, this activity will develop consensus on faculty-wide support on practices for each of the expectations. List the expectations from Form 7 of each of the small groups. Do not duplicate the expectations. Just put a check mark beside duplicate ones. You may need additional space.

EXPECTATION 1 *(FORM 8: Practices from Small Group to Total Group)*

_____

Practices

_____

_____

_____

_____

_____

_____

_____

_____

_____

_____

_____

_____

_____

_____

EXPECTATION 2 *(FORM 8: Practices from Small Group to Total Group)*

Practices

_____

_____

_____

_____

_____

_____

_____

_____

_____

_____

_____

_____

_____

_____

_____

_____

_____

_____

_____

EXPECTATION 3 *(FORM 8: Practices from Small Group to Total Group)*

Practices

_____

_____

_____

_____

_____

_____

_____

_____

_____

_____

_____

_____

_____

_____

_____

_____

_____

_____

EXPECTATION 4 *(FORM 8: Procedures from Small Group to Total Group)*

Procedures

_____

_____

_____

_____

_____

_____

_____

_____

_____

_____

_____

_____

_____

_____

_____

Now see if you can reach consensus as a group on two to four practices that will guide your efforts in developing practices to promote civility in your school. If you are not able to do this as an entire faculty, form a team to take the recommendations from Form 8. This team will seek to develop consensus on the practices and report its findings to the entire faculty. Afterward, you can begin your work on the expectations and practices that will be modeled and developed for everyone in the school.

FORM 9—FINAL EXPECTATION AND PRACTICES

Final School Expectations and Practices

You now have your expectations and practices that will guide your school-wide efforts in modeling and promoting civility. Share these with students and parents in your school community. See comments from each and adjust, if necessary.

EXPECTATION 1 *(FORM 9: Final School Expectations and Practices)*

_____

Practices

1. _____

_____

_____

2. _____

_____

_____

3. _____

_____

_____

4. _____

_____

_____

EXPECTATION 2 *(FORM 9: Final School Expectations and Practices)*

Practices

1. _____

   _____

   _____

2. _____

   _____

   _____

3. _____

   _____

   _____

4. _____

   _____

   _____

EXPECTATION 3 *(FORM 9: Final School Expectations and Procedures)*

_____

Practices

1. _____

   _____

   _____

2. _____

   _____

   _____

3. _____

   _____

   _____

4. _____

   _____

   _____

EXPECTATION 4 *(FORM 9: Final School Expectations and Practices)*

Practices

1. _____

   _____

   _____

2. _____

   _____

   _____

3. _____

   _____

   _____

4. _____

   _____

   _____

Additional Forms to Help Focus on Developing the Civil School

The following forms are designed to help the individual teacher, a team of teachers or the entire faculty and support staff assess and enhance their understanding of the importance of classroom and school civility. Some of these forms can also be used by parents to enhance their understanding of what they can do to promote civility in the school or the home. Forms 1 and 1a can be used to develop a picture of the strengths and weaknesses regarding the climate of a school. Form 2 asks us to consider the influences, both positive and negative, that are impacting our children. This is also a good form to share with parents either through a newsletter or a school/parent meeting. Form 3 places us back in the text to re-examine some of Stephen Carter's principles of civility and to develop strategies on how a particular principle could be modeled and taught to students. Form 4 asks us to define what respecting others would look like in our school or classroom. Form 5 guides us as we examine our particular curriculum and determine what within our individual curriculums could be used to promote a greater intellectual understanding of the importance of civility. Form 6 helps us focus on service learning opportunities in the school and in the community. Form 7 helps us with quick-start suggestions. We hope you find these additional forms useful in your civility developing efforts.

FORM 1—SCHOOL CLIMATE: ATTITUDE SCALE

There are many instruments available for assessing school climate or culture. The focus in this one is on a school's climate as it relates to the school's character education efforts.

Respondent: ☐ Teacher ☐ Administrator ☐ Student ☐ Support Staff
☐ Parent ☐ Central Office Administrator
☐ Community Partner ☐ Other _____

Directions: After each statement, circle the number indicating the extent to which you agree or disagree.

5 = Strongly agree   4 = Agree   3 = Neutral   2 = Disagree   1= Strongly disagree

5 4 3 2 1	1. This school is a safe place to be.
5 4 3 2 1	2. School rules are clear and fairly applied.
5 4 3 2 1	3. Standards for student achievement are clear.
5 4 3 2 1	4. Standards for student behavior are clear.
5 4 3 2 1	5. There is mutual respect between teachers and students.
5 4 3 2 1	6. This school is free from bullying and harassment.
5 4 3 2 1	7. Students respect each other in this school.
5 4 3 2 1	8. Core values are modeled by adults in this school.
5 4 3 2 1	9. Cooperative teaching and learning strategies are used in most of the classes.
5 4 3 2 1	10. Students are engaged in this school's character education efforts.
5 4 3 2 1	11. Communication is a real problem in this school.
5 4 3 2 1	12. There are high expectations for positive student behavior.
5 4 3 2 1	13. Most classes are orderly and free of disruptions.
5 4 3 2 1	14. In this school you will find most of us using civil, positive language.
5 4 3 2 1	15. Our school's character education efforts involve parents.
5 4 3 2 1	16. This community supports the work we do to teach, learn, and practice the core values.
5 4 3 2 1	17. The cafeteria is a safe and pleasant place to eat.
5 4 3 2 1	18. There is respect for the property of others.
5 4 3 2 1	19. You won't find graffiti at this school.
5 4 3 2 1	20. Add other items. _____
5 4 3 2 1	_____

Many of the items are based on the findings and recommendations of James Leming's research work reported in *Character Education: Lessons from the Past, Models for the Future* (Camden, Me.: Institute for Global Ethics, 1993.)

Taken from Edward F. DeRoche. *Evaluating Character Development: 51 Tools for Measuring Success.* (2004) Used by permission of the Character Development Group. Chapel Hill, NC.

FORM 1a—CLIMATE PERCEPTION CHECKLIST

In this second instrument for assessing school climate as it relates to the school's character education efforts, respondents' perceptions are captured in the words they might use to characterize the climate of the school. Many of the words may represent the school's core values.

Respondent: ☐ Teacher ☐ Administrator ☐ Student ☐ Support Staff
☐ Parent ☐ Central Office Administrator
☐ Community Partner ☐ Other _____

Directions: Place a check mark at the point between the two words that represents how you feel about this school.

1.	Caring	___ ___ ___ ___ ___	Uncaring
2.	Civil	___ ___ ___ ___ ___	Uncivil
3.	Safe	___ ___ ___ ___ ___	Unsafe
4.	Warm	___ ___ ___ ___ ___	Cold
5.	Fair	___ ___ ___ ___ ___	Unfair
6.	Respectful	___ ___ ___ ___ ___	Disrespectful
7.	Responsible	___ ___ ___ ___ ___	Irresponsible
8.	Exciting	___ ___ ___ ___ ___	Dull
9.	Honest	___ ___ ___ ___ ___	Dishonest
10.	Good	___ ___ ___ ___ ___	Bad
11.	Tolerant	___ ___ ___ ___ ___	Intolerant
12.	Flexible	___ ___ ___ ___ ___	Rigid
13.	Democratic	___ ___ ___ ___ ___	Authoritarian
14.	Courteous	___ ___ ___ ___ ___	Discourteous
15.	Supportive	___ ___ ___ ___ ___	Nonsupportive

Select five of the words above that best describes this school's character education efforts. Write them here:

_____

_____

_____

_____

_____

Taken from Edward F. DeRoche. *Evaluating Character Development: 51 Tools for Measuring Success.* (2004) Used by permission of the Character Development Group. Chapel Hill, NC.

FORM 2—INFLUENCES ON THE SOCIAL/MORAL DEVELOPMENT OF CHILDREN

What are some of the positive influences on the social/moral development of children?

1. _____
2. _____
3. _____
4. _____
5. _____

What are some of the negative influences on the social/moral development of children?

1. _____
2. _____
3. _____
4. _____
5. _____

Who are some of the people/groups *responsible* for helping shape the moral and social development of children?

1. _____
2. _____
3. _____
4. _____
5. _____

FORM 3—A BROAD LOOK AT CIVILITY

On page 30 there are 15 principles of civility taken from Stephen L. Carter's book *Civility: Manners, Morals, and the Etiquette of Democracy.* Quickly look over these principles. Pick one of the principles and make some notes on how you would teach this principle to create a habit of action toward other faculty or students in your school.

Principle:

_____

_____

_____

Strategies you would utilize to teach this principle and make it a habit of action in your school.

1. _____

2. _____

3. _____

4. _____

5. _____

FORM 4—RULES AND PRACTICES TO PROMOTE CIVILITY

Take the rule "Respect others." What would respect look and sound like if adults and students in the school were being respectful toward each other? For example: Students and adults have learned to disagree with each other without becoming disagreeable.

_____

_____

_____

_____

_____

_____

_____

_____

_____

Respect Others

What specifically could you teach, model and have students/adults practice to develop the habit of being respectful toward each other: e.g., say "please," "thank you," "excuse me," "pardon me," etc.?

_____

_____

_____

_____

_____

_____

_____

_____

_____

FORM 5—USING THE CURRICULUM

On page 81, we recognize that *civilized* is defined as "**2. Showing evidence of moral and intellectual advancement: humane, ethical, and reasonable.**" What are five ways that you could use your curriculum to promote an intellectual understanding of what it means to be civilized? For example: In "Daily Oral Language" I will seek out great quotes that we can punctuate and then discuss. At times, we will interpret these quotes in our journals. A high school history class might consider a close analysis of the philosophical arguments being made in Dr. Martin Luther King's "Letter From a Birmingham Jail." A physical education teacher might offer a study of "Heroes in Athletics." This might focus on athletes who struggled to make a contribution within and outside their sport area—Jackie Robinson, Wilma Rudolph, Roberto Clemente and Pat Tillman (NFL player who joined the Army Rangers after 9/11 and was killed in Afghanistan).

_____

_____

_____

_____

_____

_____

_____

_____

_____

_____

_____

_____

_____

_____

_____

_____

_____

_____

FORM 6—BECOMING THE PEOPLE WE OUGHT TO BE

What are some of the service projects that exist within your school?

_____

_____

_____

_____

_____

_____

_____

_____

What are some of the service opportunities that exist within your community?

_____

_____

_____

_____

_____

_____

_____

_____

How can you ensure that children are learning as they are serving?
e.g., Keeping a journal of their service activities and what they are learning about themselves as the serve others

_____

_____

_____

_____

_____

_____

FORM 7—GETTING STARTED

Pages 123–134 offer 21 suggestions on getting students and adults involved in promoting civility within the school. Take a quick glance at these 21 quick-start suggestions. What two to four of these suggestions would you like to work on personally in your classroom?

_____

_____

_____

_____

_____

_____

_____

What two to four suggestions would be most helpful for a school focus?

_____

_____

_____

_____

_____

_____

_____

Bibliography

INTRODUCTION

The American Heritage Dictionary of the English Language, 4th edition (2000). Boston: Houghton Mifflin.

CHAPTER 1

Burnyeat, M. F. (1980). "Aristotle on learning to be good." In Amelie Okserberg Rorty. *Essays on Aristotle's Ethics*. Berkeley: University of California Press.

Carter, S. (1998). *Civility: Manners, Morals and Etiquette of Democracy*. New York: Harper-Perennial.

Delattre, E. (2000). Civility and the limits to the tolerable. in Leroy Rouner. *Civility*. Notre Dame: Notre Dame Press.

Farkas, S., Johnson, J., Duffett, A., & Collins, K. (2002). *Aggravating Circumstances: A Status Report on Rudeness in America*. New York: Public Agenda.

Fukuyama, F. (1999, May). The great disruption: human nature and the reconstitution of social order." The Atlantic Monthly. Vol 283. No. 5 pp. 55-80.

New World Dictionary of the American Language (1986). New York: Simon and Schuster.

Peters, R. S. (1966). *Ethics and Education*. London: George Allen and Unwin.

Plank, S., McDill, E., McPartland, J., & Jordan W. (2001). Situation and repertoire: civility, incivility, cursing and politeness in an urban high school. Teachers College Record. Volume 103 Number 3, pp. 504-524. Information cited from http://www. Tcrecord.org ID Number 10760, Date Accessed: 2/6/2003

Putnam, R. (2001). *Bowling Alone: The Collapse and Revival of American Community*. New York: Simon and Schuster.

Rest J., Narvaez, D., Bebeau, M., & Thoma, S. (1999). *Post-conventional Moral Thinking: A Neo-Kohlbergian Approach*. Mahwah, New Jersey: Lawrence Erlbaum Associates Publishers.

Ryan, K. and Bohlin, K. (1999). *Building Character in Schools*. San Francisco: Jossey Bass.

Satcher, D. (2001). *Youth Violence: A Report of the Surgeon General*. Washington, D.C. U.S. Government Documents available at http://www.surgeongeneral/gov/library/youthvolence.

Schlozman, S. (December 2002-January 2003). "To View or Not to View." *Educational Leadership*. Volume 60. Number 4. pp. 87-88.

Sommers, C. (2000) *The War Against Boys: How Misguided Feminism is Harming our Young Men*. New York: Simon and Schuster.

Taylor, C. (1991) *The Ethics of Authenticity*. Cambridge, Mass: Harvard University Press.

Wolfe, A. (2001). *Moral Freedom: The Search for Virtue in a World of Choice*. New York: W. W. Norton and Company.

CHAPTER 2

Damon, W. (1995). *Greater Expectations*. New York: Free Press.

Dewey, J. (1915). *School and Society*. Chicago: University of Chicago Press.

Goleman, D. (1995). *Emotional Intelligence*. New York: Bantam Books.

Killen, M. (1991). Social and moral development in early childhood. In W. Kurtines and J. Gerwitz, eds., *Handbook of Moral Behavior and Development*, Vol. 2, Research, pp. 115-38. Hillsdale, NJ: Erlbaum. Cited in Larry Nucci (2001) *Education in the Moral Domain*. New York: Cambridge University Press.

Rousseau, J.J. (1974). *Emile*. New York: Dutton.

CHAPTER 3

Aristotle (1941). Nichomachean Ethics in *The Basic Works of Aristotle*. New York: Random House.

Barton, P., Coley, R., & Weglinsky, H. (1998). Order in the classroom: violence, discipline and student achievement. Princeton, N.J.: Educational Testing Service.

Berkowitz, M. (2002). "The science of character education." in William Damon. *Bringing in a New Era in Character Education*. Stanford, Calif.: Hoover University Press.

Kauffman, J., Burbach, H. (1997, December). On creating a climate of classroom civility. *Phi Delta Kappan* 79, No. 4 pp. 320-325.

Kilpatrick, W. (1992). *Why Johnny Can't Tell Right From Wrong*. New York: Simon and Schuster.

Leming, J. (1993, November). In search of effective character education. *Educational Leadership* 51, No. 3: 63-71.

New World Dictionary of the American Language (1986). New York: Simon and Schuster.

Nucci, L. (2001). *Education in the Moral Domain*. New York: Cambridge University Press.

Sommers, C. (2000). *The War Against Boys: How Misguided Feminism is Harming our Young Men*. New York: Simon and Schuster.

Sweeney, J. (1988). *Tips for Improving School Climate*. Arlington, Va.: American Association of School Administrators.

Wong, H. & Wong, T. (1991). *The First Days of School*. Sunnyvale, Calif.: Harry Wong Publications.

CHAPTER 4

Abourjilie, C. (2001). *Developing Character for Classroom Success*. Chapel Hill, N.C.: Character Development Publishing.

Charney, R. (1992). *Teaching Children to Care: Management in the Responsive Classroom*. Greenfield, Mass.: Northeast Foundation for Children.

Evertson, C., Emmer, E., Clements, B., Sanford, J., Worsham, M., & Williams, E. (1981). *Organizing and Managing the Elementary School Classroom*, Austin, Texas: University of Texas, Research and Development Center for Teacher Education.

Farkas, S. & Johnson J. (1997). *Different Drummers: How Teachers of Teachers View Public Education*. New York: Public Agenda.

Marzano, R., Marzano, J., & Pickering, D. (2003). *Classroom Management that Works: Research-Based Strategies for Every Teacher*. Alexandria, Va.: Association for Supervision and Curriculum Development.

Wilson J. (1993). *The Moral Sense*. New York: Free Press.

Wong, H. & Wong, T. (1991). *The First Days of School*. Sunnyvale, Calif.: Harry Wong Publications.

CHAPTER 5

Cohen, J. J., & Fish, M. C. (1993). *Handbook of School-based Interventions: Resolving Student Problems and Promoting Healthy Educational Environments*. San Francisco: Jossey-Bass Publishers.

Curwin, R. & Mendler, A. (1988). *Discipline with Dignity*. Alexandria, Va.: Association for Supervision and Curriculum Development.

Goldstein, A. P., Harootunian, B., & Conoley, J. C. (1994). *Student Aggression: Prevention, Management, and Replacement Training*. New York: Guilford Press.

Gossen, D. (1992). *Restitution: Restructuring School Discipline*. Chapel Hill, N.C.: New View Publishing.

Marzano, R. (2003). *What Works in Schools: Translating Research Into Action*. Alexandria, Va.: Association for Supervision and Curriculum Development.

Meier, D. (1995). *The Power of Their Ideas: Lessons for America from a Small School in Harlem*. Boston: Beacon Press.

New World Dictionary of the American Language, 2nd College Edition (1986).

Stage, S.A., & Quiroz, D. R. (1997). A meta-analysis of interventions to decrease disruptive classroom behavior in public education settings. *School Psychology Review*, 26(3) 333-368.

Wilson J. (1993). *The Moral Sense*. New York: Free Press.

Wynne, E. and Ryan, K. (1997). *Reclaiming Our Schools: A Handbook on Teaching Character, Academics, and Discipline*. (2nd Edition). Upper Saddle River, N.J.: Merrill Publishing.

CHAPTER 6

Adler, M. (1982). *The Paideia Proposal*. New York: Macmillan.

Adler, M. (1983). *Paideia Problems and Possibilities*. New York: Macmillan.

Adler, M. (1984). *The Paideia Program*. New York: Macmillan.

Ball, W. & Brewer, P. (2000). *Socratic Seminars in the Block*. Larchmont, N.Y.: Eye on Education, Inc.

Berkowitz, M. (1984) Process analysis and the future of moral education. Paper presented at the Annual Meeting of AERA, New Orleans, La., April 23, 1984. Also see Berkowitz, M., and Gibbs, J. (1983). Measuring the developmental features of moral discussion. *Merrill-Palmer Quarterly*, 29(4), 399-410. The description cited in this chapter is entitled: Leading moral dilemma discussions: the questioning method. The table is found in Sprinthall N. & Sprinthall R. (1987). *Educational Psychology: A Developmental Approach*. (4th Ed). New York: Random House.

Kohlberg, L. (1958). The development of modes of thinking and choices in years 10-16. Ph.D. dissertation, University of Chicago.

Kohlberg, L. (1984). *The Psychology of Moral Development*. New York: Harper & Row.

Narvaez, D., Bock, T., Endicott, L., & Samuels, J. (1998). Moral theme comprehension in third grade, fifth grade and college students. *Reading Psychology*, 19 (2), 217-241.

Narvaez, D., Gleason, T., Mitchell, C., & Bentley, L. (1999). Moral theme comprehension in children. *Journal of Educational Psychology*, 91(3), 477-487.

Narvaez, D. (2001). Individual Differences That Influence Reading Comprehension in M. Pressley and C. Bloc (eds.), *Comprehension Instruction*. New York: Guilford Press. pp. 158-175.

Narvaez, D. (2002, June). Does reading moral stories build character? *Educational Psychology Review* 14 (2). pp. 155-171

Roberts, T. (1998). *The Power of Paideia Schools: Defining Lives Through Learning*. Alexandria, Va.: Association for Supervision and Curriculum Development.

CHAPTER 7

The American Heritage® Dictionary of the English Language, 4th edition, 2000. Boston: Houghton Mifflin.

Boyte, H. C., & Farr, J. (1996, April). The work of citizenship and the problem of service learning. Paper presented at the Wingspread Conference for Character Education and Service Learning, Racine, Wis.

Charney, R. S. (1991). *Teaching Children to Care: Management in the Responsive Classroom*. Greenfield, Mass: Northeast Foundation for Children.

Corporation for National Service Interim Report. (April, 1997). *National Evaluation of Learn and Serve America School and Community-Based Programs*, Author.

Clayton, C. J., Ballif-Spanvill, B., & Hunsaker, M.D. (2001). Preventing violence and teaching peace: A review of promising and effective antiviolence, conflict-resolution, and peace programs for elementary school children. *Applied & Preventive Psychology*, 10, 1-35.

Developmental Studies Center (1995). *Creating a Caring School Community: Ideas from the Child Development Project*. Oakland, Calif.

The Golden Rule: A Global View (2003). Chapel Hill, N.C.: Character Development Group.

Johnson, D. W., Johnson, R. T., & Holubec, E. J., (1994). *Cooperative Learning*. Alexandria, Va.: Association for Supervision and Curriculum Development.

Kagan, S., (1994). *Cooperative Learning*. San Juan Capistrano, Calif.: Resources for Teachers, Inc.

Leming, John S. (1999). Character Evaluation Associates, Final Report, The Institute for Global Ethics.

Melchior, A., & Orr, L. (1995). *Evaluation of National and Community Service Programs*, Final Report, National Evaluation of Learn and Serve-America, Prepared for Corporation for National and Community Service.

Search Institute & National Youth Leadership Council. (Winter 2000). *Generator, Journal of Service Learning and Youth Leadership*. Vol.20, No.1, Pg. 26. "The Effects of Service Learning on Middle School Students' Social Responsibility and Academic Success" Study.

Skinner, R. & Chapman, C., (1999). *Service Learning and Community Service in K-12 Public Schools*. National Center for Education Statistics.

CHAPTER 8

Brown, D. (2003). *Growing Character: 99 Successful Strategies for the Elementary Classroom*. Chapel Hill, N.C.: Character Development Group.